◆ Programming in Microsoft BASIC

Programming in Microsoft BASIC

GARY B. SHELLY
THOMAS J. CASHMAN
JAMES S. QUASNEY

SHELLY
CASHMAN
SERIES

boyd & fraser publishing company

© 1992 by boyd & fraser publishing company
A Division of South-Western Publishing Company
One Corporate Place • Ferncroft Village
Danvers, Massachusetts 01923

Developed by Susan Solomon Communications

Manufactured in the United States of America

ISBN 0-87835-931-1

1 2 3 4 5 6 7 8 9 10 BC 6 5 4 3 2

◆ CONTENTS IN BRIEF

◆ CONTENTS

INTRODUCTION TO COMPUTERS

INTRODUCTION TO DOS

◆ **PROJECT 1   Working with Files on Disks   DOS2**

◆ PROJECT 2 Managing and Organizing Files on Disks DOS25

PROGRAMMING IN MICROSOFT BASIC

◆ PROJECT 3   Decisions   MB40

◆ PROJECT 4   Interactive Programming, For Loops, and An Introduction to the Top-Down Approach   MB61

◆ PROJECT 5   Sequential File Processing   MB83

◆ **PROJECT 6   Arrays and Functions   MB99**

◆ **APPENDIX   Debugging Techniques   MB118**

 **PREFACE**

Congratulations! You are about to use a Shelly Cashman Series textbook. In doing so, you join millions of other students and instructors who have discovered why this is the best-selling computer education series of all time.

The Shelly Cashman Series offers superior materials from which to learn about computers. The series includes books on computer concepts, microcomputer applications, and introductory programming. No matter what you cover in your class, the Shelly Cashman Series provides the appropriate texts.

Traditionally bound series texts are shown in the table below. If you do not find the exact combination that fits your needs, boyd & fraser's unique Custom Editions Program allows you to choose from a number of options and create a text perfectly suited to your course. This exciting new program is explained in detail on page xiii of this preface.

Traditionally Bound Texts in the Shelly Cashman Series

Computer Concepts	*Essential Computer Concepts* *Complete Computer Concepts*
Computer Concepts Study Guide	*Workbook and Study Guide with Computer Lab Software Projects to accompany Complete Computer Concepts*
Computer Concepts and Microcomputer Applications	*Essential Computer Concepts with Microcomputer Applications: WordPerfect 5.0/5.1, Lotus 1-2-3 Release 2.2, and dBASE III PLUS* *Complete Computer Concepts and Microcomputer Applications: WordPerfect 5.1, Lotus 1-2-3 Release 2.2, and dBASE III PLUS* (also available in spiral bound edition) *Complete Computer Concepts and Microcomputer Applications: WordPerfect 5.1, Lotus 1-2-3 Release 2.2, and dBASE IV Version 1.1* (also available in spiral bound edition)
Computer Concepts and Programming	*Complete Computer Concepts and Microsoft BASIC* *Complete Computer Concepts and QuickBASIC*
Microcomputer Applications	*Learning to Use Microcomputer Applications: WordPerfect 5.1, Lotus 1-2-3 Release 2.2, and dBASE III PLUS* (also available in spiral bound edition) *Learning to Use Microcomputer Applications: WordPerfect 5.1, Lotus 1-2-3 Release 2.2, and dBASE IV Version 1.1* (also available in spiral bound edition)
Word Processing	*Learning to Use Microcomputer Applications: WordPerfect 5.1* *Learning to Use WordPerfect 4.2* (WordPerfect 4.2 Educational Version Software available) *Learning to Use Microsoft Word 5.0* *Learning to Use WordStar 6.0* (with WordStar 6.0 Academic Edition Software)
Spreadsheets	*Learning to Use Microcomputer Applications: Lotus 1-2-3 Release 2.3* *Learning to Use Microcomputer Applications: Lotus 1-2-3 Release 2.2* *Learning to Use Lotus 1-2-3 Release 2.01* *Learning to Use Microcomputer Applications: Quattro Pro 3.0* *Learning to Use Microcomputer Applications: Quattro with 1-2-3 Menus* (with Quattro Educational Version Software)
Database	*Learning to Use dBASE III PLUS* (dBASE III PLUS Educational Version Software available) *Learning to Use Microcomputer Applications: dBASE IV Version 1.1* *Learning to Use Microcomputer Applications: Paradox 3.5* (with Paradox Educational Version Software)
Programming	*Programming in Microsoft BASIC* *Programming in QuickBASIC*

CONTENT

◆ Shelly Cashman Series texts assume no previous experience with computers and are written with continuity, simplicity, and practicality in mind.

Computer Concepts

The Shelly Cashman Series computer concepts textbooks offer up-to-date coverage to fit every need. *Essential Computer Concepts* is a brief concepts text that covers the topics most commonly found in short courses on computer concepts. *Complete Computer Concepts* offers a more comprehensive treatment of computer concepts.

All Shelly Cashman Series computer concepts textbooks are lavishly illustrated with hundreds of photographs and carefully developed illustrations—features that have become a hallmark of the Shelly Cashman Series. The impact of microcomputers and the user's point of view are consistently addressed throughout these texts. In addition they include coverage of important topics to help students understand today's rapidly changing technology:

- A chapter on Management Information Systems that presents information as an asset to organizations, discusses how computer-based systems effectively manage information, and addresses recent trends in decision support and expert systems.
- An innovative approach to the phases of the Information System Life Cycle.
- Up-to-date coverage of local area networks, pen-based and notebook computers, graphic user interfaces, multimedia, object-oriented programming, page printers, and desktop publishing.

Each concepts chapter concludes with:

- A Chapter Summary to help students recall and comprehend key concepts.
- Key Terms to reinforce terminology introduced in the chapter.
- Review Questions to test students' mastery of the chapter content.
- Controversial Issues to stimulate classroom discussion and critical thinking.
- Research Projects to provide opportunity for in-depth investigation of chapter content.

Microcomputer Applications

The Shelly Cashman Series microcomputer applications textbooks include projects on DOS, word processing, spreadsheets, and database management. In each project students learn by way of a unique and time-tested problem-solving approach, in which problems are presented and then *thoroughly* solved in a step-by-step manner. Numerous, carefully labeled screens and keystroke sequences illustrate the exact order of operations. Using this approach, students are visually guided as they perform the various commands and quickly come up to speed.

The DOS materials are divided into two projects. Project 1 covers the essential commands on file management and Project 2 presents directory and subdirectory file management concepts.

Each word processing application contains six projects. After an introduction to the keyboard, students are guided through the word processing cycle—starting the software, creating a document, entering text, saving, viewing, printing, and exiting to DOS. To reinforce their understanding of the cycle, students restart the software, retrieve the document they created, revise the document, save the changes, print the document, and exit to DOS again. In subsequent projects students learn to use the speller and thesaurus; to format, move, search, and replace text; to merge documents, create footnotes, and to use windows. They learn these skills by creating memos, letters, reports, and resumes.

Each spreadsheet application contains six projects. In Project 1 students learn spreadsheet terminology and basic spreadsheet characteristics and apply this know-how to create a company's first quarter sales report. In Project 2 students continue to use this sales report, learning such skills as adding summary totals, formatting, changing column widths, replication, debugging, and printing. In Project 3 students create a more complex quarterly report using what-if analysis and other skills such as inserting and deleting rows and columns, changing default settings, and copying absolute cell addresses. Projects 4, 5, and 6 cover functions and macros, graphing, and database functions, respectively.

Each database application contains six projects. In Project 1 students design and create a database of employee records, which they use as an example throughout the remaining five projects. Project 2 teaches students how to display records in a database in a variety of ways and also how to use statistical functions. Sorting and report generation are taught in Project 3. Project 4 introduces the processes of adding, changing, and deleting records. Students change the structure of the employee database, and create and use indexes and views in Project 5. Finally, in Project 6 students create custom forms for data entry and learn how to generate applications.

In all of the microcomputer applications, two beneficial learning and review tools are included at the end of each project—the Project Summary, which lists the key concepts covered in the project, and the Keystroke Summary, which is an exact listing of each keystroke used to solve the project's problem.

Finally, each project concludes with a wealth of Student Assignments. These include: true/false and multiple-choice questions; exercises that require students to write and/or explain various commands; a series of realistic problems for students to analyze and solve by applying what they have learned in the project; and minicases for the database projects.

Following the last project in each application, an easy-to-use Quick Reference is included for each project. The Quick Reference is divided into three parts—the activity, the procedure for accomplishing the activity, and a description of what actually occurs when the keys are pressed.

Programming

The Shelly Cashman Series includes QuickBASIC and Microsoft BASIC programming textbooks. They are divided into six projects that provide students with knowledge that is central to a real programming environment. They present the essentials of the language as well as structured and top-down programming techniques. In each project a problem is presented and then *thoroughly* solved step by step with a program.

In Project 1 students learn the program development cycle, the basic characteristics of the programming language, and the operating environment. Project 2 presents computations, summary tools, report editing, and report printing. In Project 3 students learn about decision making. Topics include implementing If-Then-Else and Case structures, and the use of logical operators. Unlike the first three projects, which use the READ and DATA statements to integrate data into a program, Project 4 shows students how to use the INPUT statement to accomplish this task. Also included is coverage of how to use For loops to implement counter-controlled loops, and how to design top-down programs. Project 5 introduces students to creating and processing a sequential data file. In Project 6 students learn how to write programs that can look up information in tables; they are then acquainted with the most often used built-in functions and, if applicable, special variables, of the language. Finally, an appendix on debugging techniques introduces students to debugging features that are built into the language.

Each programming project includes one or more sets of Try It Yourself Exercises, paper-and-pencil practice exercises to help master the concepts presented. Each project concludes with challenging and field-tested Student Assignments. All programming assignments include a problem statement, sample input data, and sample output results. Also included is a Reference Card that lists all statements, functions, and features of the language.

SHELLY CASHMAN SERIES CUSTOM EDITIONS

The Shelly Cashman Series provides a new textbook option so flexible that you can easily put together a unique, customized computer textbook reflecting the exact content and software requirements of your course. Because all of the Shelly Cashman Series materials use a consistent pedagogy, you can easily "mix and match" them while maintaining a clear, cohesive text. It has all been designed to work together in any combination.

When you order your custom edition, you will receive individually packaged text materials that you selected for your course needs. The customized materials arrive in a sealed box together with a durable spine binding and two covers ready for your students to assemble in seconds.

Features of the custom bound editions include:

- Text that reflects the content of your course.
- Shelly Cashman Series quality, including the same full-color materials and proven Shelly Cashman Series pedagogy found in the traditionally bound books.
- Flexibility so you can also include your own handouts and worksheets.
- Affordably priced so your students receive the Custom Edition at a cost similar to the traditionally bound books.
- Guaranteed quick order processing where your materials are sent to your bookstore within forty-eight hours of receipt of your order.
- Applications materials are continually updated to reflect the latest software versions.

The materials available in the Shelly Cashman Series Custom Edition program are listed below.

Materials Available for Shelly Cashman Series Custom Editions

Concepts	*Introduction to Computers* *Essential Computer Concepts* *Complete Computer Concepts*
Operating Systems	*Introduction to DOS* (all versions using commands) *Introduction to DOS 5.0* (using menus)
Word Processing	*Word Processing Using WordPerfect 5.1* *Word Processing Using WordPerfect 4.2* *Word Processing Using Microsoft Word 5.0* *Word Processing Using WordStar 6.0*
Spreadsheets	*Spreadsheets Using Lotus 1-2-3 Release 2.3* *Spreadsheets Using Lotus 1-2-3 Release 2.2* *Spreadsheets Using Lotus 1-2-3 Release 2.01* *Spreadsheets Using Quattro Pro 3.0* *Spreadsheets Using Quattro with 1-2-3 Menus*
Database	*Database Management Using dBASE IV Version 1.1* *Database Management Using dBASE III PLUS* *Database Management Using Paradox 3.5*
Programming	*Programming in Microsoft BASIC* *Programming in QuickBASIC*

SUPPLEMENTS

◆ Ten available supplements complement the various textbooks in the Shelly Cashman Series.

Workbook and Study Guide with Computer Lab Software Projects

This highly popular supplement contains completely new activities to enhance the concepts chapters and to simulate computer applications that are not usually available to beginning students. Included for each chapter are:

- Chapter Objectives that help students measure their mastery of the chapter content.
- A Chapter Outline that guides students through the organization of the chapter.
- A Chapter Summary that helps students recall and comprehend key concepts.
- Key Terms with definitions that reinforce terminology introduced in the chapter.
- Six projects which range from self-testing on paper and communications skills activities to on-line computerized testing with self-scoring. Answers are included for all projects and exercises.

The Computer Lab Software Projects simulate the following applications in an interactive environment:

- Home banking
- Airline reservations
- On-line information services
- Electronic mail
- Desktop publishing
- Presentation graphics

Instructor's Manual to accompany the Workbook and Study Guide with Computer Lab Software Projects

The Instructor's Manual to accompany the workbook includes answers and solutions for the entire workbook, and the software for the on-line, self-testing projects as well as for the Computer Lab Software Projects.

Educational Versions of Applications Software

Free educational versions of WordPerfect 4.2, WordStar 6.0, Quattro 1.01, Paradox 2.04, and dBASE III PLUS are available to adopting institutions. This software is available for IBM or IBM compatible systems.

Instructor's Guide Including Answer Manual and Test Bank

The Instructor's Guide and Answer Manual includes Lesson Plans for each chapter or project. The Lesson Plans begin with behavorial objectives and an overview of each chapter or project to help instructors quickly review the purpose and key concepts. Detailed outlines of each chapter and/or project follow. These outlines are annotated with the page number of the text on which the outlined material is covered; notes, teaching tips, and additional activities that the instructor might use to embellish the lesson; and a key for using the Transparency Masters and/or Color Transparencies. Complete answers and solutions for all Exercises, Discussion Questions, Projects, Controversial Issues, Student Assignments, Try It Yourself Exercises, and Minicases are also included.

This manual also contains three types of test questions with answers and is a hard copy version of MicroSWAT III (see below). The three types of questions are—true/false, multiple choice, and fill-in. Each chapter or project has approximately 50 true/false, 25 multiple choice, and 35 fill ins.

MicroSWAT III

MicroSWAT III, a microcomputer-based test-generating system, is available free to adopters. It includes all of the questions from the Test Bank in an easy-to-use, menu-driven package that allows testing flexibility and customization of testing documents. For example, with MicroSWAT III a user can enter his or her own questions and can generate review sheets and answer keys. MicroSWAT III will run on any IBM or IBM compatible system with two diskette drives or a hard disk.

Transparency Masters

Transparency Masters are available for *every* illustration in all of the Shelly Cashman Series textbooks. The transparency masters are conveniently bound in a perforated volume; they have been photographically enlarged for clearer projection.

Color Transparencies

One hundred high-quality, full-color acetates contain key illustrations found in *Complete Computer Concepts*. Each transparency is accompanied by an interleaved lecture note.

Instructor's Data Disks

The Instructor's Data Disks contain the files used in the DOS projects; the letters and memos, and the final versions of documents used to teach the word processing projects; the project worksheets and Student Assignment worksheet solutions for the spreadsheet projects; the databases that students will create and use in the database Minicases; the data for the employee database example, and program solutions to all of the programming assignments.

HyperGraphics®

HyperGraphics®, a software-based, instructor-led classroom presentation system, is available to assist adopters in delivering top-notch lectures. It allows instructors to present much of the text's content using graphics, color, animation, and instructor-led interactivity. It requires an LCD projection panel, a microcomputer, and an overhead projector.

ACKNOWLEDGMENTS

The Shelly Cashman Series would not be the success it is without the contributions of many outstanding publishing professionals, who demand quality in everything they do: Jeanne Huntington, typographer; Ken Russo, Anne Craig, Mike Bodnar, John Craig and Julia Schenden, illustrators; Janet Bollow, book design and cover design; Sarah Bendersky, photo researcher; Virginia Harvey, manuscript editor; Pat Stephan, manufacturing coordinator; Greg Hadel and Tim Davis, cover photography; Becky Herrington, director of production and art coordinator; Susan Solomon, director of development; and Thomas K. Walker, publisher and vice president of boyd & fraser publishing company. We hope you will find using this text an enriching and rewarding experience.

Gary B. Shelly
Thomas J. Cashman

Programming in Microsoft BASIC

MICROSOFT BASIC PROJECTS

An Introduction to Programming in Microsoft BASIC

OBJECTIVES

You will have mastered the material in this project when you can:

◆ Outline the general steps to solving a problem

◆ Define the terms line, statement, line number, and keyword

◆ Explain what variables and constants are in programming

◆ State the purpose of the READ and DATA statements

◆ State the purpose of the CLS, END, and REM statements

◆ State the purpose of the PRINT statement

◆ State the purpose of the WHILE and WEND statements

◆ Discuss the function of the trailer record

◆ Define the term condition and list the BASIC relations

◆ Successfully use the BASIC operating environment to enter, edit, execute, and print a BASIC program

◆ State the purpose of the system commands

◆ Explain how to obtain hard-copy output

◆ Use the reference card in the back of the text

In Project 1 we provide an introduction to the principles of program design and computer programming using the BASIC programming language. BASIC was developed for the personal computer by Microsoft Corporation, one of the largest software companies in the world. Today, BASIC is one of the most widely used programming languages on personal computers.

Our approach in illustrating BASIC is to present a series of applications that can be processed using a computer. We carefully explain the input data, the output to be produced, and the processing. Through the use of a flowchart, we illustrate the program design and logic. The flowchart is followed by an explanation of the BASIC statements required to implement the logic. We then present the complete BASIC program. The program solution, when entered into the computer and executed, will produce the output from the specified input.

THE PROGRAMMING PROCESS

◆ Computer programs can vary significantly in size and complexity. A simple program may contain only a few statements. A complex program can contain hundreds and even thousands of statements. Regardless of the size of the program, it is extremely important that the task of computer programming be approached in a professional manner, as computer programming is one of the most precise of all activities.

Learning computer programming should not be approached as a trial-and-error-type activity. By carefully reviewing the sample problems, the program design, and the BASIC code we present within these projects, you should be able to write well-designed programs that produce correct output when executed on a computer.

Computer programming is not *naturally* an error-prone activity. Errors enter into the design and coding of the computer program only through carelessness or lack of understanding of the programming process. With careful study and attention to detail, you can avoid errors. Just as it is the job of the accountant, the mathematician, the engineer, and the scientist to produce correct results, it is the job of the computer programmer to produce a program that is reliable, easy to read, and produces accurate results.

The actual programming process involves the activities described in Figure 1-1. When you use this careful approach to program design and coding, you can develop programs that are easy to read, efficient, reliable, and execute properly.

STEP	DESCRIPTION
1	Define the problem to be solved precisely in terms of input, processing, and output.
2	Design a detailed logic plan using flowcharts or some other logic tool.
3	Desk check the logic plan as if you are the computer.
4	Code the program.
5	Desk check the code as if you are the computer.
6	Enter the program into the computer.
7	Test the program until it is error free.
8	Run the program using the input data to generate the output results.

FIGURE 1-1   The program development cycle

SAMPLE PROGRAM 1 — PATIENT LISTING

◆ In this first sample program we generate a patient listing on the screen. The input data consists of the series of patient records shown in Figure 1-2. Each record contains a patient name, a doctor name, and a room number.

PATIENT NAME	DOCTOR NAME	ROOM NUMBER
Tim Krel	Nance	112
Mary Lepo	Gold	102
Tom Pep	King	245
Joe Ruiz	Ward	213
EOF	End	0

FIGURE 1-2   The patient records

The data taken as a group is called a **file**. The data about a single individual is called a **record**. Each unit of data within the record is called a **field**, or **data item**. Thus, the input data consists of a file of patient records. Each record contains a patient name field, a doctor name field, and a room number field.

In the list of records in Figure 1-2, the last record contains the patient name EOF, the doctor name End, and the room number 0. This record is called a trailer record, or sentinel record. A **trailer record** is added to the end of the file to indicate when all the valid records have been processed.

The output for this sample program is a listing on the computer screen of each record in the patient file. The output listing is shown in Figure 1-3. The patient list includes the room number, the patient name, and the doctor name for each record. Notice that the sequence of the fields displayed on the screen is different from the sequence of the fields in the input record. Column headings identify each field. After all records have been processed, the message End of Patient List displays.

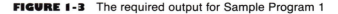

```
               Patient Listing

   Room          Patient          Doctor

   112           Tim Krel         Nance
   102           Mary Lepo        Gold
   245           Tom Pep          King
   213           Joe Ruiz         Ward

   End of Patient List
```

FIGURE 1-3   The required output for Sample Program 1

Program Flowchart

The flowchart, BASIC program, and output for Sample Program 1 are shown in Figure 1-4. The flowchart illustrates a simple looping structure. After the headings are displayed, a record is read. This read statement, prior to the loop, is called a **primary read**, or **lead read**.

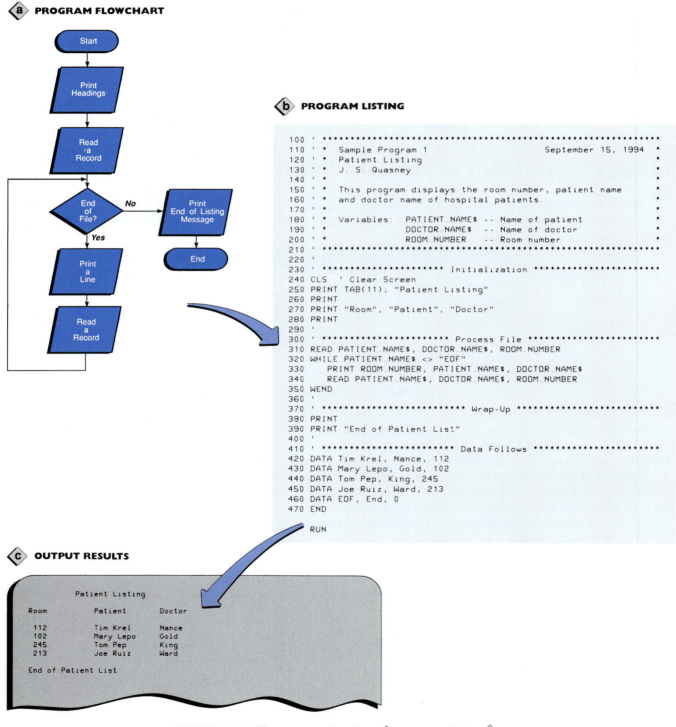

ⓐ PROGRAM FLOWCHART

ⓑ PROGRAM LISTING

```
100 ' ********************************************************
110 ' *   Sample Program 1                September 15, 1994  *
120 ' *   Patient Listing                                     *
130 ' *   J. S. Quasney                                       *
140 ' *                                                       *
150 ' *   This program displays the room number, patient name *
160 ' *   and doctor name of hospital patients.               *
170 ' *                                                       *
180 ' *   Variables:   PATIENT.NAME$ -- Name of patient       *
190 ' *               DOCTOR.NAME$  -- Name of doctor         *
200 ' *               ROOM.NUMBER   -- Room number            *
210 ' ********************************************************
220 '
230 ' ****************** Initialization ******************
240 CLS   ' Clear Screen
250 PRINT TAB(11); "Patient Listing"
260 PRINT
270 PRINT "Room", "Patient", "Doctor"
280 PRINT
290 '
300 ' ****************** Process File ******************
310 READ PATIENT.NAME$, DOCTOR.NAME$, ROOM.NUMBER
320 WHILE PATIENT.NAME$ <> "EOF"
330    PRINT ROOM.NUMBER, PATIENT.NAME$, DOCTOR.NAME$
340    READ PATIENT.NAME$, DOCTOR.NAME$, ROOM.NUMBER
350 WEND
360 '
370 ' ****************** Wrap-Up ******************
380 PRINT
390 PRINT "End of Patient List"
400 '
410 ' ****************** Data Follows ******************
420 DATA Tim Krel, Nance, 112
430 DATA Mary Lepo, Gold, 102
440 DATA Tom Pep, King, 245
450 DATA Joe Ruiz, Ward, 213
460 DATA EOF, End, 0
470 END

RUN
```

ⓒ OUTPUT RESULTS

```
        Patient Listing

Room          Patient      Doctor

 112          Tim Krel     Nance
 102          Mary Lepo    Gold
 245          Tom Pep      King
 213          Joe Ruiz     Ward

End of Patient List
```

FIGURE 1-4 The program flowchart ⓐ, program listing ⓑ, and output results ⓒ for Sample Program 1

Following the lead read in the program flowchart in Figure 1-4⟨a⟩, a test is performed to determine if the record just read was the trailer record containing the patient name EOF. If so, there are no more records to process. If not, then more records remain to be processed. This decision determines if the loop should be entered. If the end-of-file has not been reached, the loop is entered. Within the loop the previously read record is displayed on the screen and another record is read. Control then returns to the decision symbol at the top of the loop. As long as the trailer record has not been read, the looping continues.

When the trailer record is read, the looping process stops and an end-of-job message displays followed by termination of the program. This basic logic is appropriate for all applications which involve reading records and displaying the fields from the record read on an output device.

The BASIC Program

A BASIC program, such as the one in Figure 1-4⟨b⟩, is composed of a sequence of lines. Each line contains a unique line number (0 to 65529) and a statement. The **line number** serves as a label for the line which can contain up to 255 characters, although it usually contains considerably fewer. Many experienced BASIC programmers begin a program with a line number of 100 or 1000 and then increase it in each new line by 10. This leaves room to insert up to 9 extra lines at anytime. A line number must not contain any special characters such as a minus sign (–), a plus sign (+), or a decimal point (.).

Following the line number is the statement. The statement begins with a keyword. **Keywords**, such as CLS, PRINT, and READ tell the computer what to do. Keywords are often followed by a list of items needed to execute the statement. (See the last page of the reference card at the back of this book for a complete list of all the Microsoft BASIC keywords.)

The system command RUN, found just below Sample Program 1, instructs the computer to execute the program. It is not part of the program itself and, therefore, does not have a line number. For now, remember that BASIC statements have line numbers and system commands don't.

The sequence of lines that make up a BASIC program serve one of three functions:

1. Document the program
2. Cause processing to occur
3. Define data

A quality program is well documented. This means the program contains information which helps a reader understand the program. Documentation within the program should include the following:

■ A prologue, including the program name, program title, an author identification, the date the program was written, a brief description of the program, and a description of the variable names used in the program. The first 12 lines of Sample Program 1 (Figure 1-5) contain the prologue.
■ Remark lines should come before any major module in a program. In Sample Program 1, lines 230, 300, 370, and 410 are remark lines that precede major modules.

FIGURE 1-5
The prologue for Sample Program 1

```
100 ' ***********************************************************
110 ' *   Sample Program 1                    September 15, 1994 *
120 ' *   Patient Listing                                         *
130 ' *   J. S. Quasney                                           *
140 ' *                                                           *
150 ' *   This program displays the room number, patient name     *
160 ' *   and doctor name of hospital patients.                   *
170 ' *                                                           *
180 ' *   Variables:   PATIENT.NAME$ -- Name of patient           *
190 ' *                DOCTOR.NAME$  -- Name of doctor            *
200 ' *                ROOM.NUMBER   -- Room number               *
210 ' ***********************************************************
```

Documentation within a BASIC program is accomplished through the use of the REM statement. The general form of the REM statement is shown in Figure 1-6.

FIGURE 1-6
The general form of the
REM statement

REM comment

or

' comment

The remark statement begins with REM or an apostrophe (') followed by any characters, numbers, or words required to document the program. In these programming projects, we use the apostrophe (') rather than the keyword REM to initiate a remark line. Asterisks (*) are used in the remark lines to highlight the documentation.

Blank remarks, such as lines 220, 290, 360, and 400 of Sample Program 1 (Figure 1-4 ⓑ), are used to end any major module. For example, the Initialization module (Figure 1-7) begins with a remark line and ends with a blank remark line. The proper use of remark lines, blank lines, and indentations can substantially improve the readability of a program. We suggest that you follow the format illustrated in Sample Program 1 when coding all BASIC programs.

The apostrophe (') can also be used to include in-line remarks as shown following the CLS statement in line 240 of Figure 1-7. All characters that follows the apostrophe in an in-line remark are considered to be part of the documentation.

Remember that remark lines can be added before or after any line in a program. In addition, they are strictly for human comprehension and have no effect on the outcome of the program.

FIGURE 1-7
The Initialization module of
Sample Program 1

```
230 ' ******************** Initialization **********************
240 CLS   ' Clear Screen
250 PRINT TAB(11); "Patient Listing"
260 PRINT
270 PRINT "Room", "Patient", "Doctor"
280 PRINT
290 '
```

THE DATA STATEMENT

◆   Sample Program 1 employs DATA statements to define the data. The DATA statements for Sample Program 1 are shown in Figure 1-8.

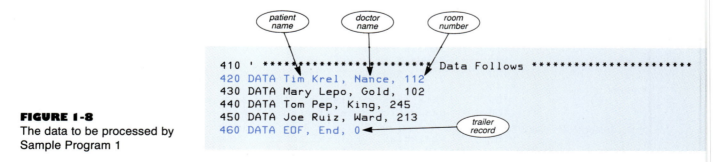

FIGURE 1-8
The data to be processed by
Sample Program 1

In Figure 1-8, line 420 defines the first patient record. Line 430 defines the second patient record, and so on. DATA statements begin with the keyword DATA followed by a space and the data. The DATA statement in line 420 contains the patient name (Tim Krel), the doctor name (Nance), and the room number (112). As shown in Figure 1-8, each of the data items must be separated by a comma.

The last DATA statement is the trailer record, when a trailer record is used in this manner, you must include an entry for each field. In line 460, the phrase EOF is included for the patient name, the word End is included in place of the doctor name, and the numeric value 0 is included for the room number. These values, of course, will not be included in the listing generated by the program.

The general form of the DATA statement is shown in Figure 1-9.

FIGURE 1-9
The general form of the
DATA statement

> DATA data item, data item, …, data item
>
> where each data item is a numeric or string value

THE CLS, PRINT, AND END STATEMENTS

◆ Up to this point, we have talked about REM and DATA statements. Both of these statements are classified as non-executable. Neither type of statement has anything to do with the logic shown in the flowchart in Figure 1-4ⓐ. For example, the DATA statements can be moved from the bottom of the program to the top of the program with no effect on the logic of the program.

In this section we discuss the CLS, PRINT, and END statements.

The CLS Statement

The first executable statement in Sample Program 1 is the CLS statement in line 240 (Figure 1-10). The function of this statement is to clear the first 24 lines of the screen and move the cursor to the upper left corner.

FIGURE 1-10
The Initialization module of
Sample Program 1

```
230 ' ********************* Initialization ************************
240 CLS  ' Clear Screen
250 PRINT TAB(11); "Patient Listing"
260 PRINT
270 PRINT "Room", "Patient", "Doctor"
280 PRINT
290 '
```

The PRINT Statement

The PRINT statement is used to write information to the screen. It is commonly used to display headings and the values of variables and control spacing in a report. As shown in its general form in Figure 1-11, the PRINT statement consists of the keyword PRINT. It may also have an optional list of print items separated by commas and semicolons.

FIGURE 1-11
The general form of the
PRINT statement

> PRINT list
>
> where **list** is the items to display separated by semicolons or commas

The list in a PRINT statement includes print items. The **print items** can be any of the following:

- Variables, such as DOCTOR.NAME$, PATIENT.NAME$, and ROOM.NUMBER
- Constants, such as numeric and string values—string values must be enclosed in quotation marks (")
- Function references, such as the TAB function—the TAB function allows you to move the cursor to the right to a specified column position

Lines 250 through 280 of Sample Program 1 (Figure 1-10) display the report title and column headings. Line 250 displays the report title on line 1. The first print item in line 250 is the TAB function. It causes the cursor to move to column 11. The semicolon following the TAB function instructs the computer to display the next print item (Patient Listing) at the current cursor location (column 11). Hence, the report title Patient Listing displays beginning in column 11 on line 1. After line 250 is executed, the cursor moves down one line on the screen to line 2.

The PRINT statement in line 260 contains no print items. A PRINT statement with no print items causes the computer to skip a line. Thus, line 2 on the screen is left blank.

Line 270 displays the three column headings. Each column heading is surrounded by the required quotation marks. Notice that the column headings also are separated by commas. When the print items are separated by commas, the fields are displayed in predefined columns called print zones. There are five print zones per line. Each **print zone** has 14 positions for a total of 70 positions per line as shown in Figure 1-12.

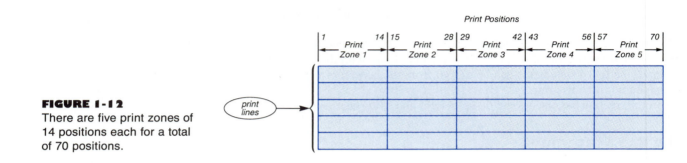

FIGURE 1-12
There are five print zones of 14 positions each for a total of 70 positions.

When line 270 in Sample Program 1 executes, Room displays beginning in column 1, Patient displays beginning in column 15, and Doctor displays beginning in column 29. Like line 260, line 280 causes the computer to skip a line on the screen.

The END Statement

The last line in Sample Program 1 is the END statement. When executed, the END statement instructs the computer to stop executing the program. Although it is not required, we recommend that you always include an END statement in your programs.

VARIABLES

In programming, a **variable** is a location in main memory whose value can change as the program executes. There are two major categories of variables—numeric and string. A **numeric variable** can only be assigned a numeric value. A **string variable** can be assigned a string of characters such as a word, name, phrase, or sentence.

A **variable name** is used to define and reference a variable in main memory. Variable names must conform to certain rules. In BASIC, a variable name begins with a letter and may be followed by up to 39 letters, digits, and decimal points. You may not use a BASIC keyword, such as CLS or PRINT, as a variable name.

String variable names always end with a dollar sign ($). Numeric variable names never end with a dollar sign. For example, in Sample Program 1, ROOM.NUMBER is a numeric variable and PATIENT.NAME$ and DOCTOR.NAME$ are string variables.

With respect to the variable names used in Sample Program 1, notice how we use the decimal point (.) to better describe what the variables will hold during the execution of the program.

THE READ STATEMENT

To assign the data in the DATA statements to variables, we use the READ statement. As shown in its general form in Figure 1-13, the READ statement consists of the keyword READ followed by one or more variable names separated from each other by commas. The variable names must be specified in the READ statement in the order in which the data is recorded in the DATA statements.

FIGURE 1-13
The general form of the
READ statement

READ variable$_1$, variable$_2$, ..., variable$_n$

where each variable is a numeric variable or string variable

When line 310 (Figure 1-14) is executed, the first data item is assigned to the first variable in the READ statement. Thus, PATIENT.NAME$ is set equal to Tim Krel, DOCTOR.NAME$ is set equal to NANCE, and ROOM.NUMBER is set equal to 112.

Refer to Sample Program 1 in Figure 1-4 ⓑ on page MB4 and notice that the READ statement in line 310 has the same number of variables as the DATA statements have data items. That is, each time a READ statement is executed, one DATA statement is used. Although we recommend this style, it is not required. For example, the following shows that it is valid to write the READ statement in line 310 as three READ statements:

```
310 READ PATIENT.NAME$
320 READ DOCTOR.NAME$
330 READ ROOM.NUMBER
340 DATA Tim Krel, Nance, 112
```

We could have also placed one data item per DATA statement as follows:

```
310 READ PATIENT.NAME$, DOCTOR.NAME$, ROOM.NUMBER
320 DATA Tim Krel
330 DATA Nance
340 DATA 112
```

THE WHILE AND WEND STATEMENTS

Following the first READ statement in line 310, lines 320 through 350 establish a **Do-While loop** (Figure 1-14). The WHILE statement in line 320 and the WEND statement in line 350 cause the range of statements between them to be executed repeatedly as long as PATIENT.NAME$ does not equal the string value EOF. In line 320 the expression PATIENT.NAME$ <> "EOF" following WHILE is called a **condition**. A condition can be true or false. In the case of the WHILE, the statements within the loop are executed while the condition is true.

FIGURE 1-14
The Process File and Wrap-
Up modules of Sample
Program 1

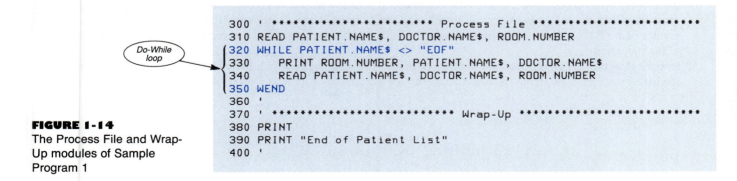

```
300 ' ********************** Process File **********************
310 READ PATIENT.NAME$, DOCTOR.NAME$, ROOM.NUMBER
320 WHILE PATIENT.NAME$ <> "EOF"
330     PRINT ROOM.NUMBER, PATIENT.NAME$, DOCTOR.NAME$
340     READ PATIENT.NAME$, DOCTOR.NAME$, ROOM.NUMBER
350 WEND
360 '
370 ' ********************** Wrap-Up **********************
380 PRINT
390 PRINT "End of Patient List"
400 '
```

Do-While
loop

When PATIENT.NAME$ does equal EOF, the condition in line 320 is false. Therefore, the computer skips the statements within the loop and continues execution at the first executable statement following the corresponding WEND statement in line 350. The first executable statement following the WEND statement is the PRINT statement in line 380.

One execution of a Do-While loop is called a **pass**. The statements within the loop, lines 330 and 340, are indented by three spaces for the purpose of readability. Collectively, lines 330 and 340 are called the **range** of statements in the Do-While loop.

Following execution of the lead read in line 310, PATIENT.NAME$ is equal to Tim Krel. Hence, control passes into the Do-While loop and the first patient record is displayed due to the PRINT statement in line 330. Next, the READ statement in line 340 assigns the variables PATIENT.NAME$, DOCTOR.NAME$, and ROOM.NUMBER the data items found in the second DATA statement. The WEND statement in line 350 automatically returns control to the WHILE statement in line 320. This process continues while PATIENT.NAME$ does not equal EOF.

The general forms of the WHILE and WEND statements are shown in Figure 1-15.

FIGURE 1-15
The general forms of the
WHILE and WEND
statements

WHILE condition

   [range of statements]

WEND

Testing for the End-of-File

Lines 420 through 450 in Sample Program 1 (Figure 1-4⟨b⟩) contain data for only four patients. The fifth patient in line 460 is the **trailer record**. It represents the end-of-file and is used to determine when all the valid data has been processed. To incorporate an end-of-file test, a variable must be selected and a trailer record added to the data. We selected the patient name as the test for end-of-file and the data value EOF. Since it guards against reading past end-of-file, the trailer record is also called the **sentinel record**. The value EOF is called the **sentinel value**. The value EOF is clearly distinguishable from all the rest of the data assigned to PATIENT.NAME$. This sentinel value is the same as the string constant found in the condition in line 320.

After the READ statement in line 340 assigns PATIENT.NAME$ the value EOF, the WEND statement returns control to the WHILE statement. Since PATIENT.NAME$ is equal to the value EOF, the WHILE statement causes the computer to pass control to line 380 which follows the corresponding WEND statement. Line 380 skips a line and line 390 displays an end-of-job message. Lines 380 and 390 are referred to as an **end-of-file routine**.

Three other worthy points to consider about establishing a test for end-of-file in a Do-While loop are:

1. It is important that the trailer record contain enough values for all the variables in the READ statement. In Sample Program 1, if we added only the sentinel value EOF to line 460, there would not be enough data to fulfill the requirements of the three variables in the READ statement. We arbitrarily assigned End and 0 to the second and third variables in the READ statement.
2. The Do-While loop requires the use of two READ statements. The first READ statement (line 310) reads the first patient record before the computer enters the Do-While loop. The second READ statement, found at the bottom of the Do-While loop (line 340), causes the computer to read the next data record. This READ statement reads the remaining data records, one at a time, until there are no more data records left. If the first record contains the patient name EOF, the WHILE statement will immediately transfer control to the statement below the corresponding WEND statement.
3. Sample Program 1 can process any number of patients by placing each in a DATA statement prior to the trailer record.

Conditions

The WHILE statement in line 320 (Figure 1-14) contains the condition

```
PATIENT.NAME$ <> "EOF"
```

The condition is made up of two expressions and a **relational operator**. The condition specifies a relationship between expressions that is either true or false. If the condition is true, execution continues with the line following the WHILE statement. If the condition is false, then control is transferred to the line following the corresponding WEND statement.

The computer makes a comparison between the two operators based on the relational operator. Figure 1-16 lists the six valid relational operators.

RELATION	MATH SYMBOL	BASIC SYMBOL	EXAMPLE
Equal To	=	=	EDUC$ = "12"
Less Than	<	<	TOTAL < 25
Greater Than	>	>	DISC > .15
Less Than Or Equal To	≤	< = or = <	DEDUC <= 10
Greater Than Or Equal To	≥	> = or = >	CODE$ >= "A"
Not Equal To	≠	< > or > <	STATE$ <> "TX"

FIGURE 1-16 Relational operators used in conditions

There are several important points to watch for in the application of conditions. For example, it is invalid to compare a numeric variable to a string value as in the following:

```
WHILE CENTS > "10"
```
this condition CENTS > "10" is invalid

Furthermore, the condition should ensure termination of the loop. For example, look at the following logical error:

```
WHILE 10 > 1
    [range of statements]
WEND
```
this condition 10 > 1 is always true

If such an error is not detected, a never-ending loop develops. There is no way to stop the endless program execution except by manual intervention, such as pressing **Ctrl + Break** on your computer keyboard. (The plus sign between two keys means hold down the first key and press the second key, and then release both keys.)

The complete BASIC program and the output results are again illustrated on the next page in Figures 1-17 and 1-18.

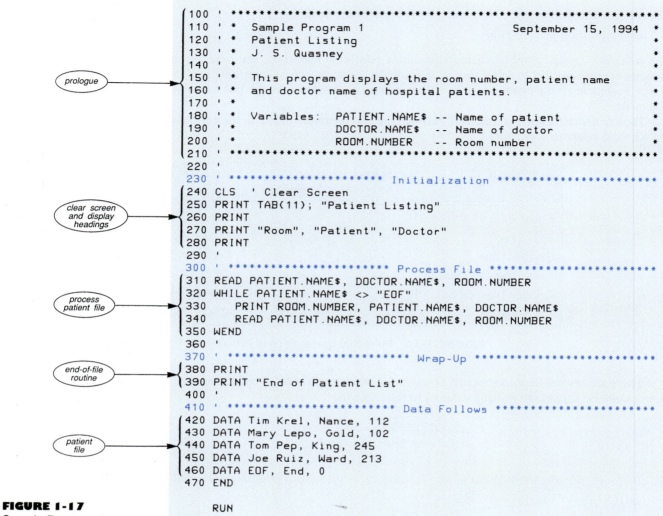

```
100 ' ************************************************************
110 ' *    Sample Program 1                    September 15, 1994  *
120 ' *    Patient Listing                                         *
130 ' *    J. S. Quasney                                           *
140 ' *                                                            *
150 ' *    This program displays the room number, patient name     *
160 ' *    and doctor name of hospital patients.                   *
170 ' *                                                            *
180 ' *    Variables:   PATIENT.NAME$ -- Name of patient           *
190 ' *                 DOCTOR.NAME$  -- Name of doctor             *
200 ' *                 ROOM.NUMBER   -- Room number                *
210 ' ************************************************************
220 '
230 ' ******************** Initialization ********************
240 CLS  ' Clear Screen
250 PRINT TAB(11); "Patient Listing"
260 PRINT
270 PRINT "Room", "Patient", "Doctor"
280 PRINT
290 '
300 ' ******************** Process File ********************
310 READ PATIENT.NAME$, DOCTOR.NAME$, ROOM.NUMBER
320 WHILE PATIENT.NAME$ <> "EOF"
330    PRINT ROOM.NUMBER, PATIENT.NAME$, DOCTOR.NAME$
340    READ PATIENT.NAME$, DOCTOR.NAME$, ROOM.NUMBER
350 WEND
360 '
370 ' ************************ Wrap-Up ************************
380 PRINT
390 PRINT "End of Patient List"
400 '
410 ' ********************* Data Follows *********************
420 DATA Tim Krel, Nance, 112
430 DATA Mary Lepo, Gold, 102
440 DATA Tom Pep, King, 245
450 DATA Joe Ruiz, Ward, 213
460 DATA EOF, End, 0
470 END

RUN
```

Labels pointing to the program:
- prologue → (lines 100–210)
- clear screen and display headings → (lines 240–280)
- process patient file → (lines 310–350)
- end-of-file routine → (lines 380–390)
- patient file → (lines 420–460)

FIGURE 1-17
Sample Program 1

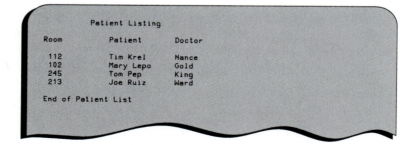

```
          Patient Listing

Room         Patient       Doctor

 112         Tim Krel      Nance
 102         Mary Lepo     Gold
 245         Tom Pep       King
 213         Joe Ruiz      Ward

End of Patient List
```

FIGURE 1-18
The output results due to
the execution of Sample
Program 1

STARTING AND QUITTING A BASIC SESSION

◆ To enter a program such as Sample Program 1 into the computer and execute it, you must familiarize yourself with how to start and quit BASIC.

Starting a Session

Boot the computer using the steps outlined by your instructor, or those found in the computer's Operations manual. Once the DOS prompt displays, enter the command BASICA. A few seconds will elapse while the BASIC program loads into main memory.

The BASIC Screen and Program Entry

After BASIC is loaded, it is automatically executed and the screen shown in Figure 1-19 displays. You can immediately begin entering your program via the keyboard. Each time you press a key on the keyboard, the corresponding character displays on the screen at the location of the cursor. The **cursor** is a movable, blinking marker on the screen that indicates where the next point of character entry, change, or display will be. When you first enter BASIC, the cursor is positioned on the screen just below the word Ok.

The top screen in Figure 1-20 shows Sample Program 1 entered. BASIC programs are entered one line at a time into the computer via the keyboard. You press the Enter key to signal the completion of a line. Typing the system command RUN instructs BASIC to execute the current program. The program displays the report shown in the bottom screen of Figure 1-20.

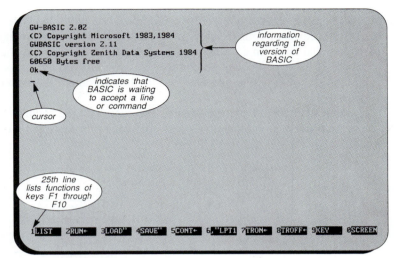

FIGURE 1-19 The initial screen that displays when you enter the command BASICA at the DOS prompt

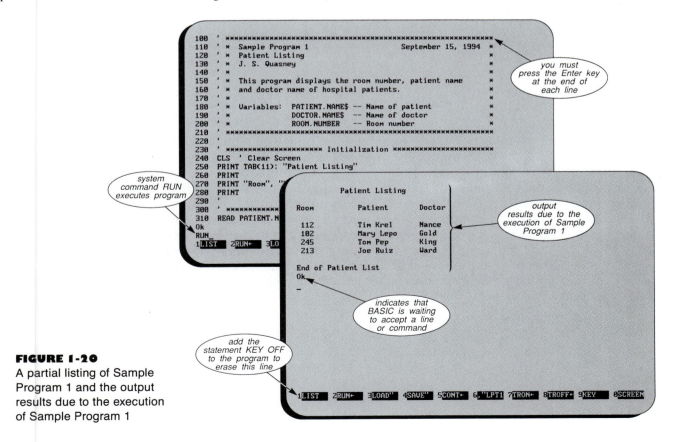

FIGURE 1-20

A partial listing of Sample Program 1 and the output results due to the execution of Sample Program 1

Quitting a BASIC Session

To quit BASIC and return control to DOS, enter the command SYSTEM. Before quitting BASIC, you should save the current program to disk for future use. The **current program** is defined as the one displaying on the screen. Shortly, we will discuss how to save a program to disk.

EDITING BASIC PROGRAMS

◆ During the process of entering a program, you will quickly learn that it is easy to make keyboard and grammatical errors because of your inexperience with the BASIC language and your unfamiliarity with the keyboard. Logical errors can also occur in a program if you have not considered all the details associated with the problem.

Some of these errors can be eliminated if you use coding forms and flowcharts and if you carefully review your design and program before you enter it into the computer. Any remaining errors are resolved by **editing** the BASIC program.

Several methods let you easily move the cursor on the screen. The most popular method of cursor movement is to use the four arrow keys located between the typewriter keys and the numeric keypad (Figure 1-21).

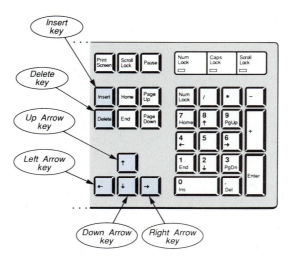

FIGURE 1-21   The arrow keys on the keyboard

Older keyboards do not include a separate set of arrow keys. With these older keyboards, the arrow keys are part of the numeric keypad. If you are using a keyboard without the separate arrow keys, then you must make sure that the Num Lock key is disengaged.

Each time you press the Delete key, the computer erases the character on which the cursor is positioned. The Backspace key erases the character to the left of the cursor.

The Insert key places the computer in **Insert mode** and allows you to insert characters at the current cursor position. As you enter characters, existing ones are *pushed* to the right. To change back to **Overtype mode**, press any arrow key or the Insert key again. There are several other special keys that you can use to edit a BASIC program. These keys are summarized on page R.4 of the Reference Card at the back of the book.

Figure 1-22 illustrates the features used most commonly in editing a BASIC program. You will find these features both powerful and easy to use.

FEATURE	INSTRUCTIONS
1. Correct an error in the line being keyed before the Enter key is pressed	Use the ← and → keys to move to the left and right within a line. You can also insert characters between any two adjacent characters by first pressing the Insert key. Or, Press the Enter key and reenter the entire line.
2. Replace a line in an existing program	Key in the new statement, using the line number of the line to be replaced. Or, Use the ↑ or ↓ key to position the cursor on the line to be replaced and follow the instructions in number 1. Be sure to press the Enter key when you are finished editing the line.
3. Insert a new line in an existing program	Key in the statement, using a line number that will cause BASIC to place the statement in the desired sequence.
4. Delete a line in an existing program	Key in the line number of the line to be deleted and press the Enter key.
5. Delete a sequence of lines	Enter the system command DELETE, followed by the beginning line number and ending line number separated by a hyphen. For example, DELETE 250-370.
6. Copy or move a line	Use the arrow keys to move the cursor to the line number of the line to be copied or moved. Change the line number to one that will position the line at the desired location and press the Enter key. This will copy the line at the new location. If it is a move operation, use number 4 to delete the unwanted line.
7. Add, delete, or change characters in a line previously entered	Move the cursor to the line to be edited and follow the instructions in number 1. Be sure to press the Enter key when you are finished editing the line.

FIGURE I-22 Commonly used features in editing BASIC programs

Often Used System Commands

As we indicated, two types of instructions are used with BASIC. One type consists of BASIC statements, like LET, PRINT, and INPUT. The second type consists of the system commands, like RUN and SYSTEM. Before we discuss system commands, it is important that you understand the concept of a file specification.

File Specifications   Several system commands require the use of a **file specification**. A file specification, also called a **filespec**, is used to identify programs and data files that are placed in auxiliary storage. A filespec is made up of a **device name**, a **file name**, and an **extension**, all included with quotation marks, as shown below.

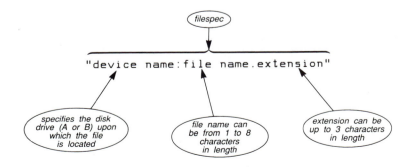

The device name refers to the disk drive, where A identifies the left-hand drive and B identifies the right-hand drive — or the top and bottom drives, respectively. BASIC programs are usually stored on disk drive B. If no device is specified, then the filespec refers to the default drive of the computer at the time of execution. If a device name is included in the file specification, it must be followed by a colon.

File names can be anywhere from 1 to 8 characters in length. Valid characters are uppercase or lowercase A–Z, 0–9, and certain special characters ($ & # @ ! % " ( ) – { } _ / \). If an extension is used, then the file name must be followed by a period.

An extension that is up to 3 characters in length can be used to classify a file. Valid characters are the same as for a file name. With BASIC, the default extension is BAS. That is, when you use system commands that refer to files, BASIC will automatically append an extension of BAS if one is not included. However, it is possible to reference programs without ever using an extension.

Examples of valid filespecs include B:PAYROLL, B:PRG-1.BAS, Accounts, and S123. The first two examples reference files on drive B. The last two examples reference files on the default drive. The computer does not differentiate between the uppercase and the lowercase characters. That is, B:PRG-1.BAS and b:prg-1.bas refer to the same file.

The RUN Command   Perhaps the most important system command for a beginner is RUN. If this command is not issued, the BASIC program will not execute. It is possible to initiate execution at a line number other than the lowest in a program. Although the system command

    RUN

instructs the computer to execute the current program in main memory beginning at the lowest line number, the command

    RUN 200

instructs the computer to execute the program beginning at line 200. What do you think happens if you enter RUN 200 and there is no line 200 in the program?

A third form of the RUN command loads and executes a program that is stored in auxiliary storage. The following,

    RUN "b:prg-1

causes the computer to load prg-1 into main memory from drive B and executes prg-1. At the time the command is issued, the current program in main memory is erased.

The LIST Command   Another useful system command is LIST. It instructs the computer to display all or part of the BASIC program. This command is especially useful in those circumstances where changes have been made to statements in the BASIC program and you want a new listing of the program.

The command LIST can be used to list lines from a point other than the first line of the program. LIST 130 lists line 130 only. LIST 110-130 lists lines 110 through 130, inclusive. To list from the start of the program through line 120, use LIST-120. Use LIST 120- to list from line 120 to the end of the program.

Pressing **Ctrl + Num Lock** causes the computer to temporarily stop an activity like a program listing. Pressing any key thereafter (except Shift, Break, and Insert) causes the computer to continue an activity like the listing of a program. Pressing Ctrl + Break causes the computer to permanently stop a program listing.

Listing Program Lines to the Printer   If you have a printer connected to your computer, you can list all or parts of your program to the printer by using the command LLIST. The command LLIST is similar to the LIST command. The only difference is that LIST displays the lines on the screen and LLIST displays the lines on the printer.

Listing Program Lines to a File   The LIST command can be used to copy lines from the current program in main memory to a file in auxiliary storage. For example,

    LIST 110-130, "b:prg-2

will copy lines 110 through 130 to the file prg-2 on drive B. The command

    LIST, "b:prg-2

will store the entire program in main memory on drive B under the name prg-2.

The NEW Command Another command that is of considerable importance is NEW. It instructs the computer to erase or delete the current program in main memory. The NEW command does not affect any BASIC program in auxiliary storage. Without this command, statements from the old program could mix with the statements of the new one.

Figure 1-23 summarizes the system commands most often used.

SYSTEM COMMAND	SHORTCUT KEYS	FUNCTION
LIST	F1	Causes all or part of the BASIC program currently in main memory to be displayed on the screen. The LIST command can also be used to copy lines to a file in auxiliary storage.
LLIST	L and F1	Causes all or part of the BASIC program currently in main memory to be displayed on the printer.
NEW		Causes the BASIC program currently in main memory to be erased and indicates the beginning of a new program to be created in main memory.
RUN	F2	Causes the BASIC program currently in main memory to be executed. This command can also be used to begin execution at a specified line number of the program in main memory or to load and execute a program from auxiliary storage.
SYSTEM		Causes the computer to permanently exit BASICA and returns control to the operating system DOS.

FIGURE 1-23 Summary of the most often used system commands

Use of the Function Keys and the KEY Statement The computer has ten **function keys** which are located above the typewriter keys or on the left side of the typewriter keys. Each function key is assigned a sequence of characters that is displayed on the twenty-fifth line of the screen when the computer is running under BASIC. This is shown in the bottom screen of Figure 1-20 on page MB13. When you press one of the function keys, its assigned sequence of characters is entered into the computer. For example, if you press F1, the system command LIST is displayed on the screen and is entered into the computer. Pressing F2 is the same as keying in the command RUN and pressing the Enter key.

The twenty-fifth line on the screen, containing the description of the function keys, can be erased through the use of the KEY statement. For example,

```
100 KEY OFF
```

instructs the computer to erase the twenty-fifth line. To redisplay the line, use the following statement:

```
200 KEY ON
```

This statement is most frequently used in tandem with the CLS statement to completely clear the screen. For example,

```
300 CLS : KEY OFF  ' Clear Screen
```

The first statement in line 300 clears the first 24 lines. The second statement clears the twenty-fifth line. The apostrophe indicates that a comment follows. Notice that it is valid to place multiple statements on the same line, provided you separate the statements with a colon (:).

The KEY statement is often entered without a line number. Any statement entered without a line number is executed immediately; it is not made part of the current program. Entering a statement without a line number is called **Immediate mode**. For example,

```
KEY OFF
```

immediately erases the twenty-fifth line. Likewise,

```
KEY ON
```

immediately displays the function of the 10 keys on the twenty-fifth line.

Additional System Commands

The system commands summarized on the previous page in Figure 1-23 are the ones most commonly used by BASIC programmers. Additional system commands that you will have to become familiar with are listed in Figure 1-24.

SYSTEM COMMAND	SHORTCUT KEYS	FUNCTION
AUTO number, increment	Alt + A	Automatically starts a BASIC line with a line number. Each new line is assigned a systematically incremented line number. Pressing Ctrl + Break terminates the AUTO activity.
CLEAR		Assigns all numeric variables the value zero and all string variables the null value.
CONT	F5	Resumes a system activity, like the execution of a program, following interruption due to pressing Ctrl + Break or execution of the STOP or END statement.
DELETE lineno$_1$,–lineno$_2$	Alt + D	Deletes lines lineno$_1$ through lineno$_2$ in the current program.
EDIT line number		Displays a line for editing purposes.
FILES "device name:		Lists the names of all programs and data files in auxiliary storage.
KILL "filespec		Deletes a previously stored program or data file from auxiliary storage.
LOAD "filespec	F3	Loads a previously stored program from auxiliary storage into main memory.
MERGE "filespec		Merges the lines from a program in auxiliary storage with the program in main memory. The program in auxiliary storage must have been saved in character format (ASCII) with the A parameter.
NAME "old filespec" AS "new filespec"		Changes the name of a program or data file in auxiliary storage to a new name.
RENUM start,,increment		Renumbers the entire program uniformly.
SAVE "filespec	F4	Saves the current program into auxiliary storage for later use. The command SAVE "filespec", A saves the file in character format (ASCII) instead of binary format.
SHELL		Places the current BASICA session in a temporary wait state and returns control to the operating system. When the operating system prompt appears, you can enter DOS commands. To return to the BASICA session, type EXIT.
TRON	F7	Turns on the program trace feature (see the Appendix).
TROFF	F8	Turns off the program trace feature (see the Appendix).

NOTE: It is not required to end the filespec with a quotation mark unless the system command requires additional information following the filespec.

FIGURE 1-24 Summary of additional system commands

The LOAD and SAVE Commands Programs are not always completed during a single session with the computer. Through the use of the SAVE and LOAD commands, it is possible with BASIC to store an incomplete program in auxiliary storage and at a later time retrieve the program. The SAVE command allows you to save BASIC programs into auxiliary storage for later use. The LOAD command allows you to load BASIC programs from auxiliary storage into main memory. Figure 1-25 shows examples of the use of these two commands.

The FILES Command   The FILES command is used to display the names of the files (both programs and data files) that are stored on the diskette in drive A or B. The following command, entered in uppercase or lowercase, displays the names of all the files stored on the diskette in drive A, which is assumed to be the default drive:

FILES   or   FILES "a:

The following command displays the names of the files on the diskette in drive B:

FILES "b:

The quotation mark preceding the device name B and the colon following it are required punctuation. Figure 1-25 shows additional examples of the FILES command.

The AUTO Command   Another important command in Figure 1-24 is the AUTO command. It is used primarily when you first enter a program. It will automatically display the next line number and, therefore, can save keying time. For example, if you enter

AUTO 100, 10

the computer will automatically display line 100. Once you complete the line and press the Enter key, the computer will display 110 on the following line. It will continue to display line numbers, incrementing each by 10, until you press Ctrl + Break.

SYSTEM COMMAND WITH FILESPEC	COMMENT
FILES "b:spa*.bas	Lists all files whose names begin with SPA and have an extension of BAS stored on the diskette in drive B. The **asterisk** (*) is called a **wild character** in programming.
FILES "b:*.bas	Lists the names of all files with an extension of BAS stored on the diskette in drive B.
LOAD "b:payroll	Loads a program named PAYROLL.BAS, stored on the diskette in drive B, into main memory.
LOAD "spa1-1	Loads a program named SPA1-1.BAS, stored on the diskette in the default drive, into main memory.
SAVE "b:spa3-2	Saves the current program in main memory on the diskette in drive B in binary format under the name SPA3-2.BAS.
SAVE "b:spa5-3", a	Saves the current program in main memory on the diskette in drive B in character format (ASCII) under the name SPA5-3.BAS.
NOTE: It is not required to end the filespec with a quotation mark unless the system command requires additional information following the filespec.	

FIGURE 1-25   Examples of system commands with file specifications

Hard-Copy Output

Most BASIC programmers use a keyboard for input and a monitor for output. In many instances, it is desirable to list the program and the results on a printer. A listing of this type is **hard-copy output**. To obtain a listing on the printer of the program itself, use the system command LLIST.

To obtain a listing of both the program and output results, press Ctrl + Print Screen, and enter the system commands LIST and RUN, as follows:

Press Ctrl + Print Screen
LIST
RUN
Press Ctrl + Print Screen again

Ctrl + Print Screen serve as a toggle. Pressing the two keys once instructs the computer to direct output to the printer as well as to the screen. Pressing the two keys following the completion of an operation instructs the computer to terminate transmission to the printer.

Sometimes you might want to obtain a hard copy of exactly what is on the screen. To do this, simply press Shift + Print Screen. The computer will print the contents of the screen, starting with line 1. This activity can easily be observed by following the movement of the cursor.

TRY IT YOURSELF EXERCISES

1. Which of the following are valid numeric variables in BASIC?
   a. X$
   b. ACCOUNT
   c. 8T
   d. INVENTORY.NO

2. Write a CLS statement and a series of PRINT statements that display the value LINE 1 beginning in column 1 of line 1, LINE 3 in column 1 of line 3, and LINE 5 in column 1 of line 5.

3. Write a PRINT statement that displays the string values NAME, ACCOUNT, BALANCE, DATE in print zones 1 through 4 of the current line.

4. Use the TAB function in a PRINT statement to display the string value The answer is beginning in column 42 of the current line.

5. Given the following DATA statement:

   DATA 16723, 12, 56

   Use the variables INVENTORY.NUMBER, ON.ORDER, and ON.HAND to write a READ statement that assigns INVENTORY.NUMBER the value 16723, ON.ORDER the value 12, and ON.HAND the value 56.

6. State the purpose of the WEND statement.

7. List and describe the six relational operators.

8. Which of the following are invalid WHILE statements? Why?
   a. 800 WHILE X = 10
   b. 810 WHALE ACCT$ <> "End"
   c. 820 WHILE 5 < TAX
   d. 830 WHILE ON.HAND LT 25
   e. 840 WHILE VOLTS EQUALS 37

9. Determine whether these conditions are true or false, given the following: Hours = 6, Tonnage = 12.5, and Bonus = 1.75
   a. HOURS >= 10
   b. TONNAGE >= 12
   c. BONUS <> 2
   d. HOURS <> 6
   e. TONNAGE < 12.5
   f. BONUS = 1.75

10. Which of the following are invalid line numbers for BASIC programs?

    a. 3 1/2   f. 100033
    b. 10   g. 1,000
    c. 9999.   h. 10.
    d. 0   i. +10
    e. 1,321   j. -10

11. Explain in one sentence the purpose of pressing Ctrl + Break.
12. Explain in one sentence each the purpose of the following system commands: AUTO, FILES, LIST, NEW, RUN, and RENUM.
13. How would you delete line 150 from the current program?
14. Is it possible to issue a RUN command more than once for the same program?
15. In a BASIC program, how do you instruct the computer to display two consecutive blank lines?
16. Write the BASIC code for the Process File and Wrap-Up modules that correspond to the following program flow-chart. Use the variable names specified in the Read and Print symbols. Do not include any DATA statements. Start each module with a remark line and end each module with a blank line. For the end-of-file test, assume the trailer record includes the following data items: EOF, 0, 0.

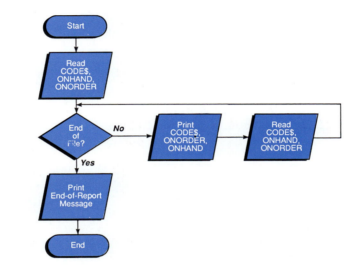

STUDENT ASSIGNMENTS

STUDENT ASSIGNMENT 1: Personnel Report

Instructions: Design and code a program using BASIC to produce the personnel listing as shown under OUTPUT. The listing includes the employee name, department number, and pay rate for each employee shown under INPUT. Submit a program flowchart, listing of the program, and a listing of the output results. To obtain a hard copy of the program and output results, use the steps described at the bottom of page MB19.

INPUT: Use the following sample data:

OUTPUT: The following results are displayed:

NAME	DEPT. NO.	PAY RATE
Sue Long	10	4.25
Chin Song	12	5.15
Mary Lopez	14	4.75
Jan Honig	14	3.85
EOF	99	9.99

```
        Personnel Report

Dept.          Name          Pay Rate

  10          Sue Long        4.25
  12          Chin Song       5.15
  14          Mary Lopez      4.75
  14          Jan Honig       3.85

End of Personnel Report
```

STUDENT ASSIGNMENT 2: Club Membership Report

Instructions: Design and code a program using BASIC to produce the club membership listing shown under OUT-PUT. The listing includes a name, birth date, and age for each member shown under INPUT. Submit a program flow-chart, listing of the program, and a listing of the output results. To obtain a hard copy of the program and output results, use the steps described at the bottom of page MB19.

INPUT: Use the following sample data:

BIRTH DATE	AGE	NAME
December 7	41	John Sutherlin
March 16	38	Jim Wachtel
June 9	27	Mary Hathaway
August 6	25	Louise Scott
EOF	99	End

OUTPUT: The following results are displayed:

```
         Membership Listing

Name:          John Sutherlin
Birth Date:    December 7
Age:              41

Name:          Jim Wachtel
Birth Date:    March 16
Age:              38

Name:          Mary Hathaway
Birth Date:    June 9
Age:              27

Name:          Louise Scott
Birth Date:    August 6
Age:              25

End of Membership Listing
```

MICROSOFT BASIC

PROJECT 2

Basic Arithmetic Operations and Accumulating Totals

OBJECTIVES

You will have mastered the material in this project when you can:

◆ State the purpose of the LET statement

◆ List the hierarchy of operations for arithmetic operators in a numeric expression

◆ Describe the effect of parentheses in the evaluation of numeric expressions

◆ Describe the use of accumulators such as counters and running totals

◆ Write elementary string expressions

◆ Explain how the PRINT USING statement is used to format output

◆ State the purpose of the LPRINT and LPRINT USING statements

Many applications require that arithmetic operations be performed on the input data to produce the required output. BASIC includes the following basic arithmetic operators: addition (+), subtraction (–), multiplication (∗), division (/), and raising a value to a power (^). These operators are similar to those used in ordinary mathematics. The operators and an example of their use in a LET statement are illustrated in Figure 2-1.

MATHEMATICAL OPERATION	BASIC ARITHMETIC OPERATOR	EXAMPLE
Addition	+	300 LET TOT = S1 + S2
Subtraction	–	350 LET PRO = PR – 5.95
Multiplication	∗	400 LET GR = HRS ∗ RATE
Division	/	450 LET AMT = COST / 5
Raising to a Power	^	500 LET DISC = RATE ^ 2

FIGURE 2-1 BASIC arithmetic operators

THE LET STATEMENT

◆ The LET statement is used to assign a variable a value. As shown in its general form in Figure 2-2, the first entry in a LET statement is the keyword LET. The keyword LET is followed by a variable name, an equal sign, and an expression.

LET numeric variable = numeric expression

   or

LET string variable = string expression

FIGURE 2-2 The general form of the LET statement

Expressions

An **expression** can be numeric or string. A **numeric expression** consists of one or more numeric constants, numeric variables, and numeric function references, all of which are separated from each other by parentheses and arithmetic operators. A **string expression** consists of one or more string constants, string variables, and string functions separated by the concatenation operator (+), which combines two strings into one. A numeric expression can only be assigned to a numeric variable. A string expression can only be assigned to a string variable.

Figure 2-3 illustrates numeric expressions in LET statements. Figure 2-4 illustrates string expressions in LET statements.

VALUE OF	LET STATEMENT	RESULTS IN
A = 15 B = 10	400 LET F = A + B - 10	F = 15
J = 32 H = 16	450 LET L = J * 2 - H	L = 48
P = 14 Y = 7	500 LET Q = P / Y	Q = 2
W = 4 S = 6	550 LET T = 6 * (S - W)	T = 12

FIGURE 2-3   Numeric expressions in LET statements

VALUE OF	LET STATEMENT	RESULTS IN
X$ = ABC	600 LET W$ = "DEF" + X$	W$ = DEFABC
F$ = WATER G$ = WINE	650 LET A$ = F$ + " INTO " + G$	A$ = WATER INTO WINE
S$ = "TOP"	700 LET S$ = S$ + "IT"	S$ = TOPIT

FIGURE 2-4   String expressions in LET statements

From the examples in Figures 2-3 and 2-4 you can see that when performing arithmetic operations, the calculations are specified to the right of the equal sign. The variable assigned the result of the expression is placed to the left of the equal sign.

Order of Operations

When multiple arithmetic operations are included in a LET statement, the **order of operations** follows the normal algebraic rules. That is, the operations are completed in the following order:

■ First, raising to a power (exponentiation) is performed from left to right.
■ Next, multiplication and division are performed from left to right.
■ Finally, addition and subtraction are performed from left to right.

For example, the expression 27 / 3 ^ 2 + 4 * 3 is evaluated as follows:

$$27 / 3 \wedge 2 + 4 * 3 = 27 / 9 + 4 * 3$$
$$= 3 \qquad + 4 * 3$$
$$= 3 \qquad + 12$$
$$= 15$$

If you had trouble following the logic behind this evaluation, use the following technique. Whenever a numeric expression is to be evaluated, *scan* from left to right three different times. On the first scan, every time you encounter an ^ operator, you perform exponentiation. In this example, 3 is raised to the power of 2, yielding 9.

On the second scan, moving from left to right again, every time you encounter the operators * and /, perform multiplication and division. Hence, 27 is divided by 9, yielding 3, and 4 and 3 are multiplied, yielding 12.

On the third scan, moving again from left to right, every time you detect the operators + and –, perform addition and subtraction. In this example, 3 and 12 are added to form 15. Thus, the following LET statement

```
200 LET AMOUNT = 27 / 3 ^ 2 + 4 * 3
```

assigns 15 to the variable AMOUNT.

The expression below yields the value of –19.37, as follows:

$$4 - 3 * 4 / 10 \wedge 2 + 5 / 4 * 3 - 3 \wedge 3 = 4 - 3 * 4 / 100 + 5 / 4 * 3 - 27$$
$$= 4 - 0.12 + 3.75 - 27$$
$$= -19.37$$

Hence, the following LET statement

```
300 LET TOTAL = 4 - 3 * 4 / 10 ^ 2 + 5 / 4 * 3 - 3 ^ 3
```

assigns –19.37 to the variable TOTAL.

The Use of Parentheses in an Expression

Parentheses may be used to change the order of operations. In BASIC, parentheses are normally used to avoid ambiguity and to group terms in a numeric expression; they do not imply multiplication. When parentheses are inserted into an expression, the part of the expression within the parentheses is evaluated first, and then the remaining expression is evaluated according to the order of operations.

If the first example contained parentheses, as does (27 / 3) ^ 2 + 4 * 3, then it would be evaluated in the following manner:

$$(27 / 3) \wedge 2 + 4 * 3 = 9 \wedge 2 + 4 * 3$$
$$= 81 + 4 * 3$$
$$= 81 + 12$$
$$= 93$$

Use parentheses freely when you are in doubt as to the formation and evaluation of a numeric expression. For example, if you want to have the computer divide 9 * TAX by 3 ^ PAYMENT, the expression may correctly be written as 9 * TAX / 3 ^ PAYMENT, but you may also write it as (9 * TAX) / (3 ^ PAYMENT) and feel more certain of the result.

For more complex expressions, BASIC allows parentheses to be contained within other parentheses. When this occurs, the parentheses are said to be **nested**. In this case, BASIC evaluates the innermost parenthetical expression first and then goes on to the outermost parenthetical expression. Thus, $(27 / 3) \char94 2 + (5 * (7 + 3))$ is broken down in the following manner:

$$
\begin{aligned}
(27 / 3) \char94 2 + (5 * (7 + 3)) &= 9 \char94 2 + (5 * (7 + 3)) \\
&= 81 + (5 * 10) \\
&= 81 + 50 \\
&= 131
\end{aligned}
$$

SAMPLE PROGRAM 2 — AUTO EXPENSE REPORT

The following sample program generates an auto expense report. The program performs calculations and accumulates totals using LET statements. Input consists of auto expense records that contain an employee name, the license number of the employee's car, the beginning mileage for the employee's car, and the ending mileage for the car. The auto expense file that will be processed by the sample program is shown in Figure 2-5.

NAME	LICENSE	BEGINNING MILEAGE	ENDING MILEAGE
T. Rowe	HRT-111	19,100	19,224
R. Lopez	GLD-913	21,221	21,332
C. Deck	LIV-193	10,001	10,206
B. Alek	ZRT-904	15,957	16,419
EOF	End	0	0

FIGURE 2-5 The employee auto expense file for Sample Program 2

The output generated by Sample Program 2 is a report displayed on the screen. The report contains the employee name, the automobile license number, the total mileage, and the expense. The total mileage is calculated by subtracting the beginning mileage from the ending mileage. The expense is calculated by multiplying the mileage by twenty-five cents.

The report contains both report headings and column headings. After all records have been processed, the total number of employees and total auto expenses are displayed. In addition, the average expense per employee is calculated by dividing the total auto expense by the total number of employees. The average expense per employee is then displayed followed by an end-of-report message. The format of the output is shown in Figure 2-6.

When using the PRINT statement, nonsignificant zeros to the right of a decimal point are not printed. For example, Alek's expense displays as 115.5 rather than 115.50. In addition, when printing decimal numbers, the numbers are left-aligned under the column heading rather than right-aligned. The single space displayed to the left of each number means that the number is positive. These factors are illustrated in the output in Figure 2-6. Later in this section, we discuss the PRINT USING statement, which allows you to adjust the values displayed to include nonsignificant zeros and right-align numeric values under the column headings.

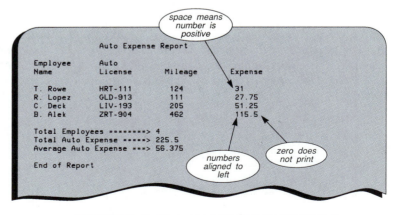

FIGURE 2-6 The report for Sample Program 2

Accumulators

Most programs require **accumulators**, which are used to develop totals. Accumulators are initialized to a value of zero in the Initialization module, then incremented within the loop in the Process File module, and finally manipulated or displayed in the Wrap-Up module. Although BASIC automatically initializes numeric variables to zero, good programming practice demands that this be done in the program. There are two types of accumulators: counters and running totals.

A **counter** is an accumulator that is used to count the number of times some action or event is performed. For example, appropriately placed within a loop, the statement

```
470 LET TOTAL.EMPLOYEES = TOTAL.EMPLOYEES + 1
```

causes the counter TOTAL.EMPLOYEES to increment by 1 each time a record is read. Associated with a counter is a statement placed in the Initialization module which initializes the counter to some value. In most cases the counter is initialized to zero.

A **running total** is an accumulator that is used to sum the different values that a variable is assigned during the execution of a program. For example, appropriately placed within a loop, the statement

```
500 LET TOTAL.EXPENSE=TOTAL.EXPENSE+AUTO.EXPENSE
```

causes TOTAL.EXPENSE to increase by the value of AUTO.EXPENSE. TOTAL.EXPENSE is called a running total. If a program is processing an employee file and the variable AUTO.EXPENSE is assigned the employee's auto expense each time a record is read, then variable TOTAL.EXPENSE represents the running total of the auto expense of all the employees in the file. As with a counter, a running total must be initialized to some predetermined value, such as zero, in the Initialization module.

Program Flowchart

The flowchart for the sample program, which produces an auto expense report and accumulates and prints final totals, is illustrated in Figure 2-7.

Prior to the loop in the flowchart, the screen is cleared, the accumulators are initialized, the headings are displayed, and the first employee record is read. Within the loop, the employee counter is incremented, the beginning mileage is subtracted from the ending mileage, giving the mileage driven by the employee. The auto expense is then calculated by multiplying the mileage driven times the auto cost per mile (.25). The auto expense is then added to the total auto expense accumulator. Next, a line of information is displayed. At the bottom of the loop another record is read. Control then returns to the top of the loop to determine if the trailer record was read. This looping process continues until there are no more auto expense records.

When the trailer record is read, the total number of employees and total auto expenses are displayed. Next, the total auto expense is divided by the total number of employees to give the average auto expense. Finally, the average and an end-of-report message are displayed.

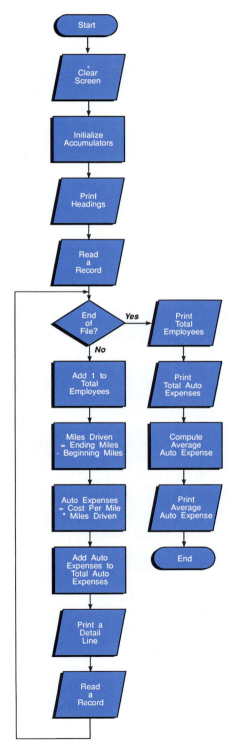

FIGURE 2-7 The flowchart for Sample Program 2

The BASIC Program

The first section of the BASIC program includes the initial documentation. As shown in Figure 2-8, the documentation is similar to Sample Program 1.

```
100 ' **********************************************************
110 ' *   Sample Program 2                    September 15, 1994  *
120 ' *   Auto Expense Report                                     *
130 ' *   J. S. Quasney                                           *
140 ' *                                                           *
150 ' *   This program displays an auto expense report.  Mileage  *
160 ' *   expense is calculated on the basis of 25 cents per mile.*
170 ' *   As part of the Wrap-Up module, the total number of      *
180 ' *   employees, total auto expense, and the average expense  *
190 ' *   per employee are displayed.                             *
200 ' *                                                           *
210 ' *   Variables:  EMP.NAME$        -- Name of employee        *
220 ' *               LICENSE$         -- Auto license number     *
230 ' *               BEGIN.MILEAGE    -- Beginning mileage       *
240 ' *               END.MILEAGE      -- Ending mileage          *
250 ' *               MILES.DRIVEN     -- Miles driven            *
260 ' *               COST.PER.MILE    -- Auto cost per mile      *
270 ' *               AUTO.EXPENSE     -- Auto expense            *
280 ' *               TOTAL.EMPLOYEES  -- Number of employees     *
290 ' *               TOTAL.EXPENSE    -- Total auto expense      *
300 ' *               AVERAGE.EXPENSE  -- Average auto expense    *
310 ' **********************************************************
320 '
```

FIGURE 2-8
The initial documentation for Sample Program 2

The DATA Statements   The DATA statements in Figure 2-9 correspond to the employee auto expense file described in Figure 2-5 on page MB26.

```
640 ' *********************** Data Follows ***********************
650 DATA T. Rowe, HRT-111, 19100, 19224
660 DATA R. Lopez, GLD-913, 21221, 21332
670 DATA C. Deck, LIV-193, 10001, 10206
680 DATA B. Alek, ZRT-904, 15957, 16419
690 DATA EOF, End, 0, 0
700 END
```

FIGURE 2-9
The DATA statements for Sample Program 2

Initialization Module   Following the initial program documentation shown in Figure 2-8, the Initialization module initializes the accumulators to zero and displays the report title and column headings. The Initialization module is shown in Figure 2-10.

```
330 ' ********************* Initialization ***********************
340 CLS : KEY OFF   ' Clear Screen
350 LET TOTAL.EMPLOYEES = 0
360 LET TOTAL.EXPENSE = 0
370 LET COST.PER.MILE = .25
380 PRINT TAB(15); "Auto Expense Report"
390 PRINT
400 PRINT "Employee", "Auto"
410 PRINT "Name", "License", "Mileage", "Expense"
420 PRINT
430 '
```

FIGURE 2-10
The Initialization module for Sample Program 2

Lines 350 and 360 initialize the employee counter (TOTAL.EMPLOYEES) and total auto expense running total (TOTAL.EXPENSE) to zero. When these two LET statements are executed, the zeros on the right side of the equal sign are assigned to the variables TOTAL.EMPLOYEE and TOTAL.EXPENSE. Counters and running totals should always be set to zero at the beginning of a program.

When the LET statement in line 370 is executed, the constant .25 on the right side of the equal sign is assigned to COST.PER.MILE. This variable can then be used later to compute the auto expense. The purpose of assigning 0.25 to a variable is to facilitate future changes to the program. For example, if the auto cost per mile were changed from 0.25 to 0.28, the constant value in line 370 could be changed to 0.28.

Lines 380 through 420 display the report title and column headings. The PRINT statement in line 380 displays the report title beginning in column 15. Line 390 skips a line in the report. Lines 400 and 410 display the column headings. Finally, line 420 skips a line in the report to leave space between the column headings and the first record displayed.

The Process File Module   The statements that make up the Process File module for Sample Program 2 are illustrated in Figure 2-11.

FIGURE 2-11

The Process File module for Sample Program 2

```
440 ' ********************** Process File **********************
450 READ EMP.NAME$, LICENSE$, BEGIN.MILEAGE, END.MILEAGE
460 WHILE EMP.NAME$ <> "EOF"
470    LET TOTAL.EMPLOYEES = TOTAL.EMPLOYEES + 1
480    LET MILES.DRIVEN = END.MILEAGE - BEGIN.MILEAGE
490    LET AUTO.EXPENSE = COST.PER.MILE * MILES.DRIVEN
500    LET TOTAL.EXPENSE = TOTAL.EXPENSE + AUTO.EXPENSE
510    PRINT EMP.NAME$, LICENSE$, MILES.DRIVEN, AUTO.EXPENSE
520    READ EMP.NAME$, LICENSE$, BEGIN.MILEAGE, END.MILEAGE
530 WEND
540 '
```

The READ statement in line 450 assigns the data in the first DATA statement (line 650 in Figure 2-9) to EMP.NAME$, LICENSE$, BEGIN.MILEAGE, and END.MILEAGE. Next, the WHILE statement in line 460 tests to see if EMP.NAME$ is not equal to EOF. Since EMP.NAME$ does not equal EOF, control enters the loop.

The LET statement in line 470 increments the employee counter (TOTAL.EMPLOYEES). Each time this statement is executed, TOTAL.EMPLOYEES is incremented by 1. Since TOTAL.EMPLOYEES was initially set to zero (line 350 in Figure 2-10), it is equal to 1 after line 470 is executed the first time. After the statement is executed a second time, the value of TOTAL.EMPLOYEES is equal to 2. This counting continues each time through the loop. When the end-of-file is detected, the value of TOTAL.EMPLOYEES is equal to the number of records processed.

The LET statement in line 480 calculates the mileage the automobile was driven (MILES.DRIVEN) by the employee being processed by subtracting the beginning mileage (BEGIN.MILEAGE) from the ending mileage (END.MILEAGE). Line 490 computes the auto expense (AUTO.EXPENSE) by multiplying the miles the automobile was driven (MILES.DRIVEN) by the cost per mile (COST.PER.MILE). In line 370 of the Initialization module (Figure 2-10), the value 0.25 was assigned to COST.PER.MILE.

The LET statement in line 500 adds the auto expense (AUTO.EXPENSE) to the accumulator TOTAL.EXPENSE. Here again, the variable TOTAL.EXPENSE was initialized to zero. When line 500 is executed the first time, the auto expense is added to the value zero. Hence, AUTO.EXPENSE is equal to T. Rowe's auto expense after the first pass on the loop. When line 500 is executed the second time, the auto expense for R. Lopez is added to the auto expense for T. Rowe. Thus, the effect of this LET statement is to accumulate the auto expenses for all the employees.

The PRINT statement in line 510 displays the employee name, license number, miles driven, and the auto expense. Next, the READ statement in line 520 assigns the data for the second employee to EMP.NAME$, LICENSE$, BEGIN.MILEAGE, and END.MILEAGE. The WEND statement in line 530 transfers control back up to the WHILE statement in line 460. Notice that statements 470 through 520 are indented three spaces to illuminate the statements within the Do-While loop. The looping process continues until the trailer record is read, at which time control is transferred to the Wrap-Up module (line 560).

End-of-File Processing   After all the records are processed, control transfers to the PRINT statement in line 560 (Figure 2-12), which causes the computer to skip a line in the report. The next PRINT statement displays the total number of employees (TOTAL.EMPLOYEES). Notice the manner in which the PRINT statement is written to display both a constant and a variable. The phrase Total Employees ========> is enclosed within quotation marks ("). The right quotation is followed by a semicolon (;). A semicolon causes the computer to display the value of TOTAL.EMPLOYEES immediately after the phrase rather than in the next print zone. Recall that if the numeric value is positive, a blank space appears before the numeric value.

After line 580 displays the total auto expense, line 590 computes the average auto expense which is displayed by line 600. Line 610 skips a line and line 620 displays an end-of-report message. Finally, line 700 (Figure 2-9) terminates execution of the program.

```
550 ' *************************** Wrap-Up ***************************
560 PRINT
570 PRINT "Total Employees ========>"; TOTAL.EMPLOYEES
580 PRINT "Total Auto Expense =====>"; TOTAL.EXPENSE
590 LET AVERAGE.EXPENSE = TOTAL.EXPENSE / TOTAL.EMPLOYEES
600 PRINT "Average Auto Expense ===>"; AVERAGE.EXPENSE
610 PRINT
620 PRINT "End of Report"
630 '
```

FIGURE 2-12
The Wrap-Up module for
Sample Program 2

The Complete BASIC Program   The complete Sample Program 2 is illustrated in Figure 2-13. The report generated by Sample Program 2 is shown in Figure 2-14.

```
100 ' ******************************************************************
110 ' *   Sample Program 2                        September 15, 1994  *
120 ' *   Auto Expense Report                                         *
130 ' *   J. S. Quasney                                               *
140 ' *                                                               *
150 ' *   This program displays an auto expense report.  Mileage     *
160 ' *   expense is calculated on the basis of 25 cents per mile.    *
170 ' *   As part of the Wrap-Up module, the total number of          *
180 ' *   employees, total auto expense, and the average expense      *
190 ' *   per employee are displayed.                                 *
200 ' *                                                               *
210 ' *   Variables:   EMP.NAME$          -- Name of employee         *
220 ' *                LICENSE$           -- Auto license number      *
230 ' *                BEGIN.MILEAGE      -- Beginning mileage        *
240 ' *                END.MILEAGE        -- Ending mileage           *
250 ' *                MILES.DRIVEN       -- Miles driven             *
260 ' *                COST.PER.MILE      -- Auto cost per mile        *
270 ' *                AUTO.EXPENSE       -- Auto expense             *
280 ' *                TOTAL.EMPLOYEES    -- Number of employees      *
290 ' *                TOTAL.EXPENSE      -- Total auto expense        *
300 ' *                AVERAGE.EXPENSE    -- Average auto expense     *
310 ' ******************************************************************
320 '
330 ' ********************** Initialization **********************
340 CLS : KEY OFF   ' Clear Screen
350 LET TOTAL.EMPLOYEES = 0
360 LET TOTAL.EXPENSE = 0
370 LET COST.PER.MILE = .25
380 PRINT TAB(15); "Auto Expense Report"
390 PRINT
400 PRINT "Employee", "Auto"
410 PRINT "Name", "License", "Mileage", "Expense"
420 PRINT
430 '
```

FIGURE 2-13
Sample Program 2

FIGURE 2-13
(continued)

```
440 ' ********************** Process File **********************
450 READ EMP.NAME$, LICENSE$, BEGIN.MILEAGE, END.MILEAGE
460 WHILE EMP.NAME$ <> "EOF"
470    LET TOTAL.EMPLOYEES = TOTAL.EMPLOYEES + 1
480    LET MILES.DRIVEN = END.MILEAGE - BEGIN.MILEAGE
490    LET AUTO.EXPENSE = COST.PER.MILE * MILES.DRIVEN
500    LET TOTAL.EXPENSE = TOTAL.EXPENSE + AUTO.EXPENSE
510    PRINT EMP.NAME$, LICENSE$, MILES.DRIVEN, AUTO.EXPENSE
520    READ EMP.NAME$, LICENSE$, BEGIN.MILEAGE, END.MILEAGE
530 WEND
540 '
550 ' ************************* Wrap-Up *************************
560 PRINT
570 PRINT "Total Employees ========>"; TOTAL.EMPLOYEES
580 PRINT "Total Auto Expense =====>"; TOTAL.EXPENSE
590 LET AVERAGE.EXPENSE = TOTAL.EXPENSE / TOTAL.EMPLOYEES
600 PRINT "Average Auto Expense ===>"; AVERAGE.EXPENSE
610 PRINT
620 PRINT "End of Report"
630 '
640 ' ********************** Data Follows **********************
650 DATA T. Rowe, HRT-111, 19100, 19224
660 DATA R. Lopez, GLD-913, 21221, 21332
670 DATA C. Deck, LIV-193, 10001, 10206
680 DATA B. Alek, ZRT-904, 15957, 16419
690 DATA EOF, End, 0, 0
700 END

    RUN
```

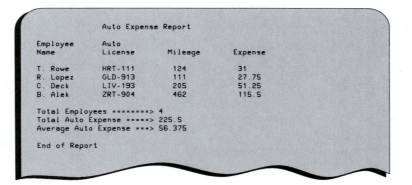

FIGURE 2-14
The output results due to the execution of Sample Program 2

REPORT EDITING

Although the output in Figure 2-14 is readable, it does not conform to the format used by business and industry. For example, a column of numeric values usually has the decimal points aligned and is right-justified under the column heading. Numeric values that represent dollars and cents should include two digits to the right of the decimal point. Placing information in a format such as this is called **report editing**.

BASIC provides for report editing through the use of the PRINT USING statement. This statement allows you to do the following:

- Specify the exact image of a line of output.
- Force decimal-point alignment when displaying numeric tables in columnar format.
- Control the number of digits displayed for a numeric result.
- Specify that commas be inserted into a number. (Starting from the units position of a number and progressing toward the left, digits are separated into groups of three by a comma.)

- Specify that the sign status of the number be displayed along with the number (+ or blank if positive, − if negative).
- Assign a fixed or floating dollar sign ($) to the number displayed.
- Force a numeric result to be displayed in exponential form.
- Left- or right-justify string values in a formatted field (that is, align the leftmost or rightmost characters, respectively).
- Specify that only the first character of a string be displayed.
- Round a value automatically to a specified number of decimal digits.

The general form of the PRINT USING statement is shown in Figure 2-15.

FIGURE 2-15
The general form of the PRINT USING statement

PRINT USING "format field"; list

or

PRINT USING string variable; list

where **format field** or **string variable** indicates the format and **list** is a variable or a group of variables separated by commas.

Report editing with the PRINT USING statement is accomplished using special characters to format the values to be displayed. When grouped together, these special characters form a **format field**. A format field is incorporated in a program as a string constant in the PRINT USING statement or as a string constant assigned to a string variable.

To illustrate the use of the PRINT USING statement, we will modify Sample Program 2. The new, formatted report is illustrated in Figure 2-16.

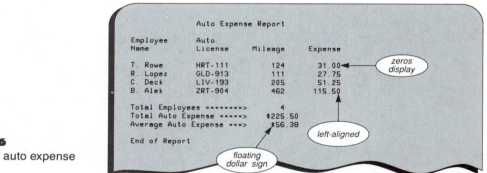

FIGURE 2-16
The formatted auto expense report

Compare the report in Figure 2-16 to the one in Figure 2-14. Notice that the mileage in the third column in Figure 2-16 is right-justified under the column heading. Also, the dollar and cents values in the expense field are right-justified under the column heading, and the decimal points are aligned. In addition, the total auto expense and the average auto expense per employee values are displayed with the dollar sign immediately adjacent to the leftmost digit in the number. This is known as a **floating dollar sign**.

To control the format of the displayed values, the PRINT USING statement is used in combination with a string expression that specifies exactly the image to which the output must conform. The string expression is placed immediately after the words PRINT USING in the form of a string constant or string variable. If the format is described by a string variable, then the string variable must be assigned the format by a LET statement before the PRINT USING statement is executed in the program. In either case, the items to display follow the string constant or string variable in the PRINT USING statement separated by commas. The two methods for specifying the format for the PRINT USING statement are shown in Figure 2-17.

Method 1:

```
490 ' Format Specified as a String in the PRINT USING Statement
500 PRINT USING "Item ### costs $$,###.##"; ITEM, COST
```

Method 2:

```
300 ' Format Specified Earlier and Assigned to a String Variable
310 D1$ = "Item ### cost $$,###.##"
    .
    .
500 PRINT USING D1$; ITEM, COST
```

FIGURE 2-17
The two methods for defining the format for a PRINT USING statement

In Method 1 of Figure 2-17, the string following the keywords PRINT USING instructs the computer to display the values of ITEM and COST using the format found in the accompanying string constant. In Method 2, the string constant has been replaced by the string variable D1$ which was assigned the desired format in a previous statement. If ITEM is equal to 314 and COST is equal to 2,145.50, then the results displayed from the execution of either PRINT USING statement in Method 1 or Method 2 are as follows:

```
Item 314 costs $2,145.50
```

In Method 2 of Figure 2-17, notice that the keyword LET is not part of the LET statement. BASIC considers any statement with an equal sign to be a LET statement. Hence, the keyword LET is optional. When defining format fields, we will not use the keyword LET.

Figure 2-18 illustrates how a LET statement and a PRINT USING statement are used to display the detail line in the report in Figure 2-16.

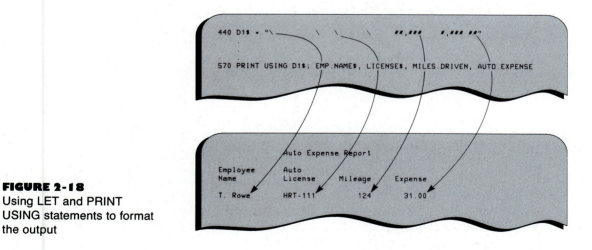

FIGURE 2-18
Using LET and PRINT USING statements to format the output

The backward slash (\) is used to create a format for string fields. The first backward slash indicates the first character position in the string field, and the second backward slash indicates the last character position in the field. Therefore, in the format field for EMP.NAME$, eleven character positions are defined—the two backward slashes and the nine spaces between them.

LICENSE$ is also a string variable. It is defined as eight characters in length by the two backward slashes and the six spaces between them. Numeric fields are defined through the use of the number sign (#). Each occurrence of a number sign corresponds to a numeric digit position. Punctuation, such as the comma and decimal point, is placed in the format field where it is to occur in the actual output. The format field for MILES.DRIVEN includes a comma in case the value exceeds 999. Since MILES.DRIVEN in the first line of the report is less than 1,000, the comma does not display. Similarly, a decimal point is placed in the format where it is supposed to print. The format field ###.## for AUTO.EXPENSE specifies three digits to the left of the decimal point and two digits to the right of the decimal point. Thus, the value displays in dollars and cents form.

Notice in Figure 2-18, following the keywords PRINT USING, D1$ identifies the format. D1$ is then followed by a semicolon, and the names of the fields to display are separated by commas. The table in Figure 2-19 illustrates additional examples of format fields.

EXAMPLE	DATA	FORMAT FIELD	RESULTS IN
1	125.62	###.##	125.62
2	005.76	###.##	bb5.76
3	.65	###.##	bb0.65
4	1208.78	#,###.##	1,208.78
5	986.05	#,###.##	bb986.05
6	34.87	$$#,###.##	bbbb$34.87
7	3579.75	$$#,###.##	b$3,579.75
8	561.93	$##,###.##	$bbb561.93
9	SALLY	\ \	SALLY
10	EDWARD	\\	ED

FIGURE 2-19 Examples of format fields (b represents a blank character)

You can include constants in a format field. The LET statement in Figure 2-20 illustrates this point.

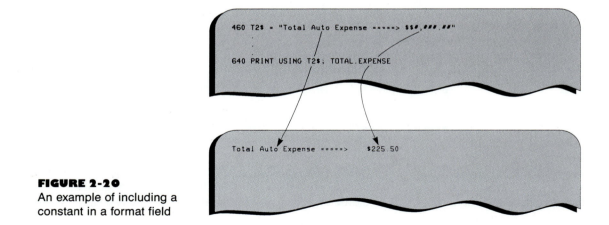

FIGURE 2-20
An example of including a constant in a format field

In Figure 2-20, the constant Total Auto Expense ======> is part of the string expression that includes the format field. When the variable T2$ is referenced by the PRINT USING statement, the constant is displayed exactly as it appears in the string expression. There are additional format symbols available with BASIC. Those we present here, however, are the most widely used.

The coding in Figure 2-21 illustrates the complete program which produces the auto expense report shown on the next page in Figure 2-22. Pay particular attention to lines 390 through 480. These lines, when grouped together, show exactly what the report will look like when the program executes. Notice that this group of lines includes PRINT statements that display the report title and column headings and LET statements that define format fields. The column headings are within one string constant, rather than separated by commas, to better control the spacing. The format fields for the detail line (D1$) are immediately below the column headings in line 440.

We did not use the keyword LET in lines 440 through 480 so that all the string constants, including those in the PRINT statements, would begin in the same column in the program.

```
100 ' ************************************************************
110 ' *   Sample Program 2 Modified              September 15, 1994  *
120 ' *   Auto Expense Report                                        *
130 ' *   J. S. Quasney                                              *
140 ' *                                                              *
150 ' *   This program displays an auto expense report.  Mileage     *
160 ' *   expense is calculated on the basis of 25 cents per mile.   *
170 ' *   As part of the Wrap-Up module, the total number of         *
180 ' *   employees, total auto expense, and the average expense     *
190 ' *   per employee are displayed.                                *
200 ' *                                                              *
210 ' *   Variables:   EMP.NAME$          -- Name of employee        *
220 ' *               LICENSE$           -- Auto license number     *
230 ' *               BEGIN.MILEAGE      -- Beginning mileage       *
240 ' *               END.MILEAGE        -- Ending mileage          *
250 ' *               MILES.DRIVEN       -- Miles driven            *
260 ' *               COST.PER.MILE      -- Auto cost per mile      *
270 ' *               AUTO.EXPENSE       -- Auto expense           *
280 ' *               TOTAL.EMPLOYEES -- Number of employees        *
290 ' *               TOTAL.EXPENSE    -- Total auto expense        *
300 ' *               AVERAGE.EXPENSE -- Average auto expense       *
310 ' *               D1$, T1$, T2$, T3$, T4$  --  Print images     *
320 ' ************************************************************
330 '
340 ' ******************** Initialization ********************
350 CLS : KEY OFF  ' Clear Screen
360 LET TOTAL.EMPLOYEES = 0
370 LET TOTAL.EXPENSE = 0
380 LET COST.PER.MILE = .25
390 PRINT "              Auto Expense Report"
400 PRINT
410 PRINT "Employee        Auto"
420 PRINT "Name            License      Mileage      Expense"
430 PRINT
440 D1$ = "\           \   \     \     ##,###     #,###.##"
450 T1$ = "Total Employees =========>    ###"
460 T2$ = "Total Auto Expense ======> $$#,###.##"
470 T3$ = "Average Auto Expense ===>   $$,###.##"
480 T4$ = "End of Report"
490 '
500 ' ******************** Process File ********************
510 READ EMP.NAME$, LICENSE$, BEGIN.MILEAGE, END.MILEAGE
520 WHILE EMP.NAME$ <> "EOF"
530    LET TOTAL.EMPLOYEES = TOTAL.EMPLOYEES + 1
540    LET MILES.DRIVEN = END.MILEAGE - BEGIN.MILEAGE
550    LET AUTO.EXPENSE = COST.PER.MILE * MILES.DRIVEN
560    LET TOTAL.EXPENSE = TOTAL.EXPENSE + AUTO.EXPENSE
570    PRINT USING D1$; EMP.NAME$, LICENSE$, MILES.DRIVEN, AUTO.EXPENSE
580    READ EMP.NAME$, LICENSE$, BEGIN.MILEAGE, END.MILEAGE
590 WEND
600 '
```

image of report

FIGURE 2-21
Sample Program 2 modified to include report editing

(continued)

FIGURE 2-21
(continued)

```
610 ' ************************** Wrap-Up **************************
620 PRINT
630 PRINT USING T1$; TOTAL.EMPLOYEES
640 PRINT USING T2$; TOTAL.EXPENSE
650 LET AVERAGE.EXPENSE = TOTAL.EXPENSE / TOTAL.EMPLOYEES
660 PRINT USING T3$; AVERAGE.EXPENSE
670 PRINT
680 PRINT T4$
690 '
700 ' ********************** Data Follows **********************
710 DATA T. Rowe, HRT-111, 19100, 19224
720 DATA R. Lopez, GLD-913, 21221, 21332
730 DATA C. Deck, LIV-193, 10001, 10206
740 DATA B. Alek, ZRT-904, 15957, 16419
750 DATA EOF, End, 0, 0
760 END

    RUN
```

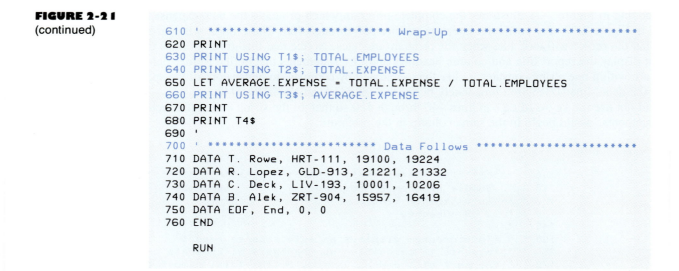

```
                Auto Expense Report

      Employee      Auto
      Name          License      Mileage      Expense

      T. Rowe       HRT-111          124        31.00
      R. Lopez      GLD-913          111        27.75
      C. Deck       LIV-193          205        51.25
      B. Alek       ZRT-904          462       115.50

      Total Employees ========>        4
      Total Auto Expense =====>   $225.50
      Average Auto Expense ===>    $56.38

      End of Report
```

FIGURE 2-22
The formatted auto expense
report due to the execution of
the modified Sample
Program 2

PRINTING A REPORT ON THE PRINTER

◆   While the `PRINT` and `PRINT USING` statements display results on the screen, the `LPRINT` and `LPRINT USING` statements print results on the printer. Everything that has been presented with respect to the `PRINT` and `PRINT USING` statements in this section applies to the `LPRINT` and `LPRINT USING` statements. Obviously, to use these statements, you must have a printer attached to your computer and it must be in Ready mode.

Figure 2-23 illustrates the results of the modified Sample Program 2 printed on a printer. To obtain the hard-copy results as shown in Figure 2-23, change all the `PRINT` and `PRINT USING` statements in Sample Program 2 (Figure 2-21) to `LPRINT` and `LPRINT USING` statements.

```
                Auto Expense Report

      Employee      Auto
      Name          License      Mileage      Expense

      T. Rowe       HRT-111          124        31.00
      R. Lopez      GLD-913          111        27.75
      C. Deck       LIV-193          205        51.25
      B. Alek       ZRT-904          462       115.50

      Total Employees ========>        4
      Total Auto Expense =====>   $225.50
      Average Auto Expense ===>    $56.38
```

FIGURE 2-23
A printed version of the auto
expense report

TRY IT YOURSELF EXERCISES

1. Which arithmetic operation is performed first in the following numeric expressions?
   a. 5 * (AMT + 8)
   b. COST - SALE + DISCOUNT
   c. 8 / 3 * 5
   d. (X * (2 + Y)) ^ 2 + Z ^ (2 ^ 2)
   e. X + Y / Z

2. Evaluate each of the following:
   a. 2 * 10 * 6 / 12 - 7 ^ 2 / 7
   b. (6 - 8) + 5 ^ 3
   c. 12 / 6 / 2 + 7 * 3 + 5

3. Calculate the numeric value for each of the following valid numeric expressions if AMT = 3, SALE = 4, COST = 5, DISCOUNT = 3, S1 = 4, S2 = 1, and S3 = 2.
   a. (AMT + SALE / 2) + 6.2
   b. 3 * (AMT ^ SALE) / COST
   c. (AMT / (COST + 1) * 4 - 5) / 2
   d. S2 + 2 * S3 * DISCOUNT / 3 - 7 / (S1 - S2 / S3) - DISCOUNT ^ S1

4. Determine the output results for each program.

   a. ```
      100 ' Exercise 4.a
      110 X = 2.5
      120 Y = 4 * X / 2 * X + 10
      130 PRINT Y
      140 Y = 4 * X / (2 * X + 10)
      150 PRINT Y
      160 X = -X
      170 PRINT X
      180 X = -X
      190 PRINT X
      200 END
      ```

   b. ```
      100 ' Exercise 4.b
      110 C = 4
      120 D = 1
      130 S = C + D
      140 PRINT S
      150 T = D - C
      160 PRINT T
      170 C = S + T - C
      180 PRINT C
      190 D = 2 * (S + T + C) / 4
      200 PRINT D
      210 END
      ```

5. Calculate the numeric value for each of the following numeric expressions if X = 2, Y = 3, and Z = 6.
   a. X + Y ^ 2
   b. Z / Y / X
   c. 12 / (3 + Z) - X
   d. X ^ Y ^ Z
   e. X * Y + 2.5 * X + Z
   f. (X ^ (2 + Y)) ^ 2 + Z ^ (2 ^ 2)

6. Insert parentheses so that each of the following results in the value indicated on the right-hand side of the arrow.
   a. 10 / 3 + 2 + 12 ----> 14
   b. 3 ^ 2 - 1 ----> 3
   c. 6 / 2 + 1 + 3 * 4 ----> 4

7. For each of the format fields and corresponding data in the table to the right, indicate what the computer displays. Use the letter b to indicate the space character. Notice that if a format field does not include enough positions to the left of the decimal point, the computer displays the result preceded by a percent (%) sign. If the format field does not include enough positions to the right of the decimal point, the computer rounds the result to fit the format field.

FORMAT FIELD	DATA	RESULT
a. ####	15	
b. #,###	345	
c. $$,###.##	1395.54	
d. ###.##	12.5675	
e. ##,###.###	19412.5	
f. ##.##	576.3	
g. ###.#####	32.2	
h. #.##	.234	

STUDENT ASSIGNMENTS

STUDENT ASSIGNMENT 1: Payroll Report

Instructions: Design and code a BASIC program to generate the formatted payroll report shown under OUTPUT. The weekly pay is calculated by multiplying the hourly pay by the number of hours. All hours are paid at straight time. As part of the Wrap-Up module, display the total number of employees and the total weekly pay of all employees. Submit a program flowchart, listing of the program, and a listing of the output results.

INPUT: Use the following sample data:

EMPLOYEE NAME	HOURLY PAY RATE	HOURS WORKED
Joe Lomax	7.70	40
Ed Mann	6.05	38.5
Louis Orr	8.10	45
Ted Simms	9.50	39.5
Joan Zang	12.00	92
EOF	0	0

OUTPUT: The following results are displayed:

```
                   Payroll Report

     Employee      Hourly      Hours       Weekly
     Name          Rate        Worked      Pay

     Joe Lomax     7.70        40.0        308.00
     Ed Mann       6.05        38.5        232.93
     Louis Orr     8.10        45.0        364.50
     Ted Simms     9.50        39.5        375.25
     Joan Zang     12.00       92.0        1,104.00

     Total Employees ········>      5
     Total Weekly Pay ·······> $2,384.68

     End of Report
```

STUDENT ASSIGNMENT 2: Test Score Report

Instructions: Design and code a BASIC program that prints the student test report shown under OUTPUT. In each detail line, include the student's name, test scores, and average test score. The average test score is calculated by adding the score for test 1 and the score for test 2 and dividing by two. After all records for all students have been processed, print the total number of students and the class average for all tests. To obtain a class average, add all test scores and divide by twice the number of students. Use the LPRINT and LPRINT USING statements to generate the report on the printer.

INPUT: Use the following sample data:

STUDENT NAME	TEST 1 SCORE	TEST 2 SCORE
Julie Banks	70	78
John Davis	92	93
Joe Gomez	88	84
Sally Katz	78	83
EOF	0	0

OUTPUT: The following results are printed:

```
            Test Score Report

Student
Name          Test 1      Test 2      Average

Julie Banks     70          78         74.0
John Davis      92          93         92.5
Joe Gomez       88          84         86.0
Sally Katz      78          83         80.5

Total Students ------------>    4
Class Average  ------------>  83.25

End of Report
```

Decisions

OBJECTIVES

You will have mastered the material in this project when you can:

◆ State the purpose of the IF statement

◆ State the purpose of the GOTO statement

◆ Differentiate between a logical line and a physical line

◆ Identify and describe the programming logic structures; If-Then-Else and case

◆ Describe a compound condition

◆ List the order of operations for the logical operators

◆ Describe how parentheses can be used to change the order of precedence

◆ State the purpose of the ON-GOTO statement

BASIC includes the IF and ON-GOTO statements to instruct the computer to select one or more actions. You use the IF statement to implement the **If-Then-Else structure** shown in Figure 3-1. When the structure in a flowchart has more than two alternative paths and the decision is based on an integer test, you use the ON-GOTO statement. This type of structure is called a **case structure** and is shown in Figure 3-2.

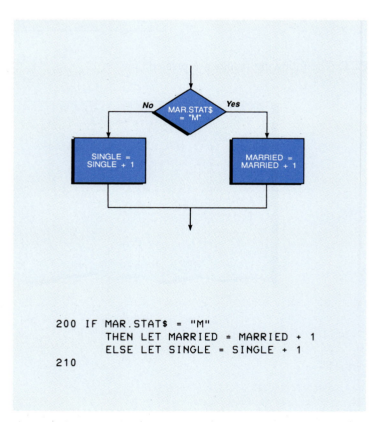

```
200 IF MAR.STAT$ = "M"
        THEN LET MARRIED = MARRIED + 1
        ELSE LET SINGLE = SINGLE + 1
210
```

FIGURE 3-1 For the If-Then-Else structure, use the IF statement

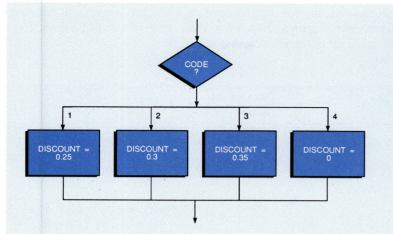

```
300 ON CODE GOTO 310, 330, 350, 370
310    LET DISCOUNT = .25
320 GOTO 380
330    LET DISCOUNT = .3
340 GOTO 380
350    LET DISCOUNT = .35
360 GOTO 380
370    LET DISCOUNT = 0
380
```

THE IF STATEMENT

The IF statement is commonly regarded as the most powerful statement in BASIC. The major function of this statement is to choose between two alternative paths. The IF statement has two general forms as shown in Figure 3-3.

> IF condition THEN true task ELSE false task
>
> or
>
> IF condition THEN true task
>
> where **condition** is a comparison between two expressions
> that is either true or false
> **true task** or **false task** is a statement,
> a series of statements, or a line number

FIGURE 3-3 The general forms of the IF statement

In Figure 3-3, if the condition is true, the computer executes the true task, also called the THEN clause, or **true case**. If the condition is false, the computer executes the false task, also called the ELSE clause, or **false case**. After either case is executed, control passes to the next numbered line following the IF statement. If the true or false task is a line number, then control passes to the specified line number.

Six types of relations can be used in a condition within an IF statement. These relations include determining if:

1. One value is equal to another (=)
2. One value is less than another (<)
3. One value is greater than another (>)
4. One value is less than or equal to another (< =)
5. One value is greater than or equal to another (> =)
6. One value is not equal to another (< >)

Recall that these are the same six relational operators we discussed earlier with the WHILE statement in Project 1 on page MB11 in Figure 1-16.

Figure 3-4 illustrates several examples of IF statements with conditions made up of numeric and string expressions. For numeric conditions, the computer evaluates not only the magnitude of each resultant expression but also its sign. For string expressions, the computer evaluates the two strings from left to right, one character at a time. Examples 1 through 3 in Figure 3-4 include conditions made up of numeric expressions. Examples 4 and 5 show IF statements with conditions made up of string expressions.

EXAMPLE	STATEMENT	VALUE OF VARIABLES	RESULT
1	```100 IF AMT = 0 THEN LET DIS = 4``` ```110```	AMT = 0	The condition is true. The variable DIS is set equal to 4 and control passes to line 110.

2	```200 IF A >= B```
	``` THEN PRINT X : LET T = T + 10```
	``` ELSE PRINT Y : LET TAX = TAX + 5```
	```210```
		A = 3
		B = 5
			The condition is false. The value of Y is displayed; TAX is incremented by 5; and control passes to line 210.

3	```300 IF F > X - Y - 6 THEN 350```
	```310 LET CNT = CNT + 1```
	```320 PRINT F, X, Y```
	```330 READ F, X, Y```
	```340 GOTO 370```
	```350 LET DEFCNT = DEFCNT + 1```
	```360 READ F, X, Y```
	```370```
		F = 23
		X = 7
		Y = −8
			The condition is true. Control passes to line 350; DEFCNT is incremented by 1; and F, X, and Y are assigned values. Control passes to line 370.

4	```400 IF C$ < D$ + E$```
	``` THEN READ A, B, C : PRINT Y```
	```410```
		C$ = "JIM"
		D$ = "JA"
		E$ = "MES"
			The condition is false. Control passes to line 410.

5	```500 IF X$ = "YES" THEN PRINT A$``` ```510```	X$ = "yes"	The condition is false. Control passes to line 510.

FIGURE 3-4 Examples of IF statements

Notice the programming style used to write the code in Example 2 of Figure 3-4. The THEN and ELSE clauses are on separate lines without line numbers. Furthermore, for the sake of readability, the keywords THEN and ELSE are indented three spaces in relation to the keyword IF. This programming style will be used to write most of the IF statements in these projects. To write IF statements using this style, you must understand the difference between logical lines and physical lines.

Logical versus Physical Lines

BASIC differentiates between a **logical line** and a **physical line**. A logical line is composed of a line number that is followed by one or more physical lines that have no line numbers. Each logical line can contain up to 255 characters (254 plus the Enter key). Each physical line, except for the last, contains 80 characters. The last physical line contains the exact number of characters displayed and the Enter key. Therefore, a logical line can have a maximum of four physical lines. The last physical line can have up to 15 characters.

To terminate a physical line with fewer than 80 characters displayed, press Ctrl + Enter. This combination of keys causes the computer to fill the remainder of the physical line with blank characters and to move the cursor to column 1 of the next physical line. You end the last physical line by pressing the Enter key. Consider again Example 2 in Figure 3-4:

```
200 IF A >=B
        THEN PRINT X : LET T = T + 10
        ELSE PRINT Y : LET TAX = TAX + 5
210
```

The logical line 200 is made up of three physical lines. The first two physical lines are terminated by pressing Ctrl + Enter. The last line is terminated by pressing the Enter key.

GOTO — A Dangerous Four-Letter Word

As with most programming languages, BASIC includes the infamous GOTO statement. The GOTO statement unconditionally transfers control to the line number following the keyword GOTO.

The GOTO statement can be used to transfer control backward or forward to any line in the same program. In other words, you can instruct the computer to jump around from one routine to another without any return. Overuse of the GOTO statement can result in inefficient and unreliable code that is difficult to follow and difficult to maintain.

Use the GOTO statement only in combination with the IF and ON-GOTO statements. And then use it only to branch forward to a higher line number. With the IF statement, use it only when the true and false tasks involve several statements and it improves the readability of the program. Consider Example 3 in Figure 3-4. In our opinion the multiple lines and the GOTO statement make the code easier to read. The alternative is to write the code as one line by separating the statements in each task with the colon (:) in the following way:

```
300 IF F > X - Y - 6
        THEN LET CNT = CNT + 1 : PRINT F, X, Y : READ F, X, Y
        ELSE LET DEFCNT = DEFCNT + 1 : READ F, X, Y
310
```

We recommend that when there is more than two statements in either the THEN or ELSE clause, you use multiple lines and the GOTO statement (Example 3, Figure 3-4) rather than one line as shown above.

CODING IF-THEN-ELSE STRUCTURES

◆ This section describes various forms of the If-Then-Else structure and the use of IF statements to implement them in BASIC.

Simple If-Then-Else Structures

Consider the If-Then-Else structure shown on the next page in Figure 3-5 and the corresponding methods of implementing the logic in BASIC. Assume that the variable AGE represents a person's age. If AGE is greater than or equal to 18, the person is an adult. If AGE is less than 18, the person is a minor. ADULT and MINOR are counters that are incremented as specified in the flowchart.

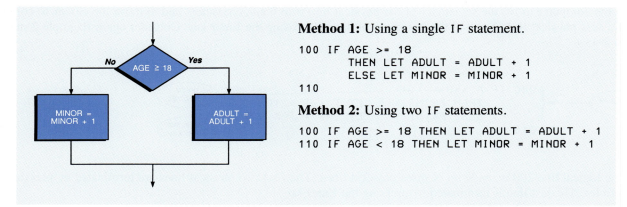

Method 1: Using a single IF statement.

```
100 IF AGE >= 18
        THEN LET ADULT = ADULT + 1
        ELSE LET MINOR = MINOR + 1
110
```

Method 2: Using two IF statements.

```
100 IF AGE >= 18 THEN LET ADULT = ADULT + 1
110 IF AGE < 18 THEN LET MINOR = MINOR + 1
```

FIGURE 3-5 Coding an If-Then-Else structure with alternative processing for the true and false cases

In Method 1 in Figure 3-5, an IF statement resolves the logic indicated in the partial flowchart. Line 100 compares AGE to 18. If AGE is greater than or equal to 18, then ADULT is incremented by 1. If AGE is less than 18, the false task is carried out and MINOR is incremented by 1. Regardless of the counter incremented, control passes to line 110.

In Method 2, two single-line IF statements are used. AGE is compared to the value 18 twice. In the first IF statement, the counter ADULT is incremented by 1 if AGE is greater than or equal to 18. In the second IF statement, the counter MINOR is incremented by 1 if AGE is less than 18.

Although both methods are valid and both satisfy the If-Then-Else structure, the first method is more efficient, as it involves fewer lines of code and less execution time. Therefore, the first method is recommended over the second.

As shown in Figures 3-6, 3-7, and 3-8, the If-Then-Else structure can take on a variety of appearances. In Figure 3-6, there is a task only if the condition is true. The first method of implementation is preferred over the second since it is more straightforward and less confusing. In Method 2 of Figure 3-6, we reversed the relation. Although this method satisfies the If-Then-Else structure, it is also more difficult to understand. The second method shows that it is valid to have a null THEN clause.

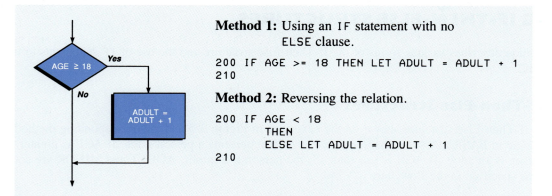

Method 1: Using an IF statement with no ELSE clause.

```
200 IF AGE >= 18 THEN LET ADULT = ADULT + 1
210
```

Method 2: Reversing the relation.

```
200 IF AGE < 18
        THEN
        ELSE LET ADULT = ADULT + 1
210
```

FIGURE 3-6 Coding an If-Then-Else structure with alternative processing for the true case

The If-Then-Else structure in Figure 3-7 illustrates the incrementation of the counter MINOR when the condition is false. In Method 1, the relation in the condition that is found in the partial flowchart has been reversed. The condition AGE >= 18 has been modified to read AGE < 18 in the BASIC code. Reversing the relation is usually preferred when additional tasks must be done as a result of the condition being false. In Method 2, the relation is the same as in the decision symbol. When the condition AGE >= 18 is true, the null THEN clause simply passes control to line 310. Either method is acceptable. Some programmers prefer always to include both a THEN and an ELSE clause, even when one of them is null; whereas, others prefer to reverse the relation rather than include a null clause.

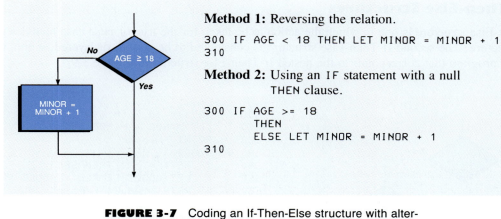

Method 1: Reversing the relation.

```
300 IF AGE < 18 THEN LET MINOR = MINOR + 1
310
```

Method 2: Using an IF statement with a null THEN clause.

```
300 IF AGE >= 18
        THEN
        ELSE LET MINOR = MINOR + 1
310
```

FIGURE 3-7 Coding an If-Then-Else structure with alternative processing for the false case

In Figure 3-8, each task in the If-Then-Else structure is made up of multiple actions. In Method 1, if the condition AGE >= 18 is true, the two statements in the THEN clause are executed. Recall that multiple statements are allowed on the same line provided they are separated by the colon (:). If the condition is false, the two statements in the ELSE clause are executed. In either case, control passes to line 410 after the task is executed.

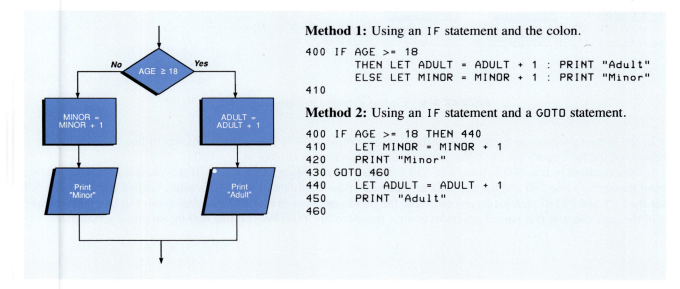

Method 1: Using an IF statement and the colon.

```
400 IF AGE >= 18
        THEN LET ADULT = ADULT + 1 : PRINT "Adult"
        ELSE LET MINOR = MINOR + 1 : PRINT "Minor"
410
```

Method 2: Using an IF statement and a GOTO statement.

```
400 IF AGE >= 18 THEN 440
410     LET MINOR = MINOR + 1
420     PRINT "Minor"
430 GOTO 460
440     LET ADULT = ADULT + 1
450     PRINT "Adult"
460
```

FIGURE 3-8 Coding an If-Then-Else structure with several statements for both the true and false cases

In Method 2 of Figure 3-8, the statements that make up the true and false tasks are on separate lines. The true task is made up of lines 440 and 450. The false task is made up of lines 410 and 420. If the condition is true in line 400, then control transfers to line 440 (true task). Following execution of the true task, control passes to line 460. If the condition is false in line 400, control passes to line 410 (false task). After the false task is executed, the GOTO statement in line 430 transfers control forward around the true task to line 460.

For this particular example, we recommend that you use Method 1. However, if the number of statements in a task increases beyond two, we recommend that you use the technique shown in Method 2.

Nested If-Then-Else Structures

A nested If-Then-Else structure is one in which the action to be taken for the true or false case includes yet another If-Then-Else structure. The second If-Then-Else structure is considered to be nested, or layered, within the first. Study the partial program that corresponds to the nested If-Then-Else structure in Figure 3-9.

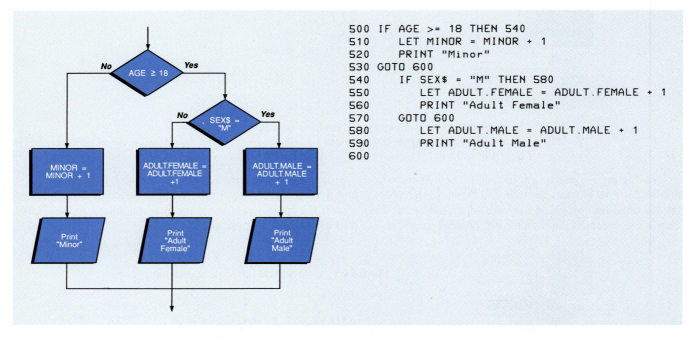

```
500 IF AGE >= 18 THEN 540
510     LET MINOR = MINOR + 1
520     PRINT "Minor"
530 GOTO 600
540     IF SEX$ = "M" THEN 580
550         LET ADULT.FEMALE = ADULT.FEMALE + 1
560         PRINT "Adult Female"
570     GOTO 600
580         LET ADULT.MALE = ADULT.MALE + 1
590         PRINT "Adult Male"
600
```

FIGURE 3-9   Coding a nested If-Then-Else structure

In the partial program in Figure 3-9, if the condition Age >= 18 is false, control passes to line 510. Following execution of the false task, the GOTO statement in line 530 transfers control to line 600.

If the condition in line 500 is true, line 540 evaluates the condition SEX$ = "M". If this second condition is true, control transfers to line 580 and the true task is executed. If the condition in line 540 is false, control passes to line 550. After the LET and PRINT statements are executed, the GOTO statement in line 570 transfers control to line 600. Regardless of the path taken in this partial program, control passes to line 600. We call line 600 the structure terminator.

SAMPLE PROGRAM 3 — VIDEO RENTAL REPORT

◆ To illustrate a program that uses an IF statement, consider the following video rental problem. In this application, if the video tape is rented for three days or less, the charge is $2.49 per day. There is a one dollar per day discount for each of the first three days for customers who are at least 65 years old. If the video tape is rented for more than three days, the charge is $3.49 per day for each day over three days.

The video records consist of the customer's name and age, the video title, and the number of days rented as shown in Figure 3-10.

CUSTOMER NAME	AGE	VIDEO TITLE	DAYS RENTED
Helen Moore	47	Lost in Space	1
Hank Fisher	67	Together Again	3
Joe Frank	34	Three Lives	7
Al Jones	64	The Last Day	5
Shirley Star	65	Monday Morning	4
EOF	0	End	0

FIGURE 3-10 The video rental file for Sample Program 3

The output is a printed video rental summary report that lists the customer name, customer age, title of the video tape rented, the number of days the tape was rented, and the charge for the rental. After all records have been processed, the number of senior citizen customers, the number of tapes rented, and the total charges are printed. The format of the output is illustrated in Figure 3-11.

```
                        Video Rental Report

        Customer               Video           Days
        Name          Age      Title           Rented      Charge

        Helen Moore    47      Lost in Space        1        2.49
        Hank Fisher    67      Together Again       3        4.47
        Joe Frank      34      Three Lives          7       17.43
        Al Jones       64      The Last Day         5       12.45
        Shirley Star   65      Monday Morning       4        5.96

        Senior Citizens ----------->       2
        Videos Rented ------------->       5
        Total Charges ------------>    $42.80

        End of Report
```

FIGURE 3-11 The report for Sample Program 3

Program Flowchart

The flowchart in Figure 3-12 illustrates the logic required to produce the video rental report.

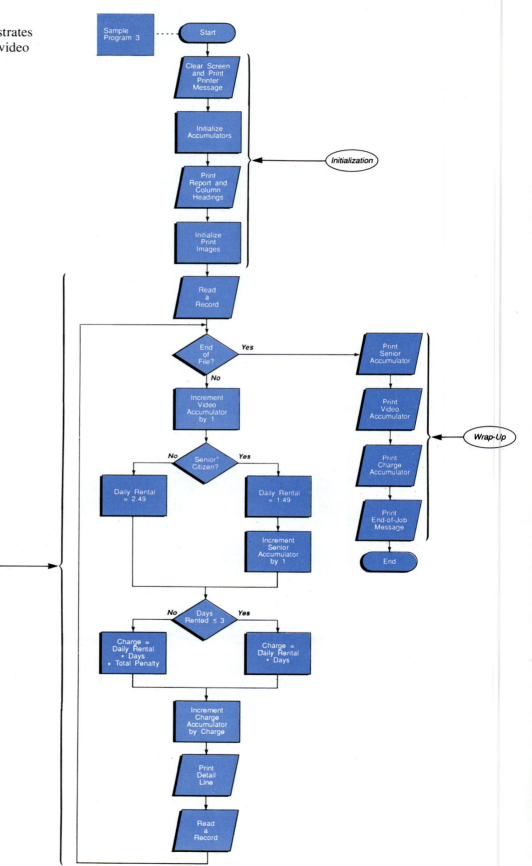

FIGURE 3-12
The flowchart for Sample Program 3

The BASIC Program

The program in Figure 3-13 corresponds to the program flowchart in Figure 3-12.

FIGURE 3-13
Sample Program 3

```
100 ' **************************************************************
110 ' *   Sample Program 3                    September 15, 1994   *
120 ' *   Video Rental Report                                      *
130 ' *   J. S. Quasney                                            *
140 ' *                                                            *
150 ' *   This program prints a video rental report.  The charge  *
160 ' *   is based on the number of days the video is rented and  *
170 ' *   the age of the customer.                                 *
180 ' *        As part of the Wrap-Up module, the total number     *
190 ' *   of videos, senior customers, and charges are printed.    *
200 ' *                                                            *
210 ' *   Variables:   CUS.NAME$        -- Name of customer         *
220 ' *               CUS.AGE          -- Customer age             *
230 ' *               VIDEO.TITLE$     -- Title of video           *
240 ' *               DAYS.RENTED      -- Days rented              *
250 ' *               DAILY.RENTAL     -- Cost per day             *
260 ' *               CHARGE           -- Cost of renting video    *
270 ' *               PENALTY          -- Cost per day after 3 days *
280 ' *               TOTAL.VIDEOS     -- Number of videos rented  *
290 ' *               TOTAL.SENIORS    -- Number of senior rentals *
300 ' *               TOTAL.CHARGES    -- Total charges            *
310 ' *               DL1$, TL1$, TL2$, TL3$, TL4$ -- Print images *
320 ' **************************************************************
330 '
340 ' ********************** Initialization **********************
350 CLS : KEY OFF    ' Clear Screen
360 PRINT "****** Video Rental Report Printing on Printer ******"
370 LET TOTAL.VIDEOS = 0
380 LET TOTAL.SENIORS = 0
390 LET TOTAL.CHARGES = 0
400 LET PENALTY = 3.49
410 LPRINT "                      Video Rental Report"
420 LPRINT
430 LPRINT "Customer               Video               Days"
440 LPRINT "Name              Age  Title                    Rented   Charge"
450 LPRINT
460 DL1$ = "\             \  ###    \                 \      ###    ###.##"
470 TL1$ = "Senior Citizens ==========>    ###"
480 TL2$ = "Videos Rented ============>    ###"
490 TL3$ = "Total Charges ============> $$,###.##"
500 TL4$ = "End of Report"
510 '
520 ' ********************* Process File *********************
530 READ CUS.NAME$, CUS.AGE, VIDEO.TITLE$, DAYS.RENTED
540 WHILE CUS.NAME$ <> "EOF"
550    LET TOTAL.VIDEOS = TOTAL.VIDEOS + 1
560    IF CUS.AGE >= 65
          THEN LET DAILY.RENTAL = 1.49 : LET TOTAL.SENIORS = TOTAL.SENIORS + 1
          ELSE LET DAILY.RENTAL = 2.49
570    IF DAY.RENTED <= 3
          THEN LET CHARGE = DAILY.RENTAL * DAYS.RENTED
          ELSE LET CHARGE = (DAILY.RENTAL*DAYS.RENTED)+PENALTY*(DAYS.RENTED-3)
580    LET TOTAL.CHARGES = TOTAL.CHARGES + CHARGE
590    LPRINT USING DL1$; CUS.NAME$, CUS.AGE, VIDEO.TITLE$, DAYS.RENTED, CHARGE
600    READ CUS.NAME$, CUS.AGE, VIDEO.TITLE$, DAYS.RENTED
610 WEND
620 '
```

(continued)

FIGURE 3-13
(continued)

```
630 ' ************************* Wrap-Up ****************************
640 LPRINT
650 LPRINT USING TL1$; TOTAL.SENIORS
660 LPRINT USING TL2$; TOTAL.VIDEOS
670 LPRINT USING TL3$; TOTAL.CHARGES
680 LPRINT
690 LPRINT TL4$
700 '
710 ' ********************* Data Follows ********************
720 DATA Helen Moore, 47, Lost in Space, 1
730 DATA Hank Fisher, 67, Together Again, 3
740 DATA Joe Frank, 34, Three Lives, 7
750 DATA Al Jones, 64, The Last Day, 5
760 DATA Shirley Star, 65, Monday Morning, 4
770 DATA EOF, 0, End, 0
780 END

    RUN
```

Discussion of Sample Program 3

When Sample Program 3 is executed, the report shown in Figure 3-14 prints on the printer. Sample Program 3 includes the following significant points that did not appear in previous programs.

■ When executed, line 350 clears the screen and line 360 displays a friendly message informing the user that the report is being printed on the printer.
■ LPRINT and LPRINT USING statements are used throughout the program to print the report on the printer rather than display the report on the monitor.
■ There are two IF statements that select alternative paths on the basis of the data in the video record being processed. The IF statement in line 560 determines whether the customer is a senior citizen. If the customer is a senior citizen, the daily rental (DAILY.RENTAL) is set to $1.49 and the senior citizen counter is incremented. If the customer is not a senior citizen, then the daily rental is set to $2.49.

The second IF statement (line 570) determines how much to charge the customer being processed. If the video is rented for three days or less, the charge is determined from the following LET statement:

```
LET CHARGE = DAILY.RENTAL * DAYS.RENTED
```

If the video is rented for more than three days, the charge is determined from the following LET statement:

```
LET CHARGE = (DAILY.RENTAL * DAYS.RENTED) + PENALTY * (DAYS.RENTED - 3)
```

```
                        Video Rental Report

Customer                Video           Days
Name            Age     Title           Rented    Charge

Helen Moore     47      Lost in Space      1       2.49
Hank Fisher     67      Together Again     3       4.47
Joe Frank       34      Three Lives        7      17.43
Al Jones        64      The Last Day       5      12.45
Shirley Star    65      Monday Morning     4       5.96

Senior Citizens ------------>     2
Videos Rented  ------------->     5
Total Charges  ------------->  $42.80

End of Report
```

FIGURE 3-14 The report printed when Sample Program 3 is executed

LOGICAL OPERATORS

◆ In many instances a decision to execute a true task or false task is based upon two or more conditions. In previous examples that involved two or more conditions, we tested each condition in a separate IF statement. In this section, we discuss combining conditions within one IF statement by means of the logical operators AND and OR. When two or more conditions are combined by these logical operators, the expression is called a **compound condition**. The logical operator NOT allows you to write a compound condition in which the truth value of the simple condition following NOT is **complemented**, or reversed.

The NOT Logical Operator

A simple condition that is preceded by the logical operator NOT forms a compound condition that is false when the simple condition is true. If the simple condition is false, then the compound condition is true. Consider the two IF statements in Figure 3-15. Both print the value of DISCOUNT if MARGIN is less than or equal to COST.

FIGURE 3-15
Use of the NOT logical
operator

Method 1: Using the NOT logical operator.

```
100   IF NOT MARGIN > COST THEN PRINT DISCOUNT
110
```

Method 2: Reversing the logical operator.

```
100   IF MARGIN <= COST THEN PRINT DISCOUNT
110
```

In Method 1 of Figure 3-15, if MARGIN is greater than COST (the simple condition is true), then the compound condition NOT MARGIN > COST is false. If MARGIN is less than or equal to COST (the simple condition is false), then the NOT makes the compound condition true. In Method 2, the relational operator is reversed and, therefore, the NOT is eliminated. Both methods are equivalent.

Because the logical operator NOT can increase the complexity of the decision statement significantly, use it sparingly. As shown in Figure 3-15, you can always reverse the relational operator in a condition to eliminate the logical operator NOT.

The AND Logical Operator

The AND logical operator requires that both conditions be true for the compound condition to be true. Consider the two IF statements in Figure 3-16. Both statements read a value for SELLING.PRICE if MARGIN is greater than 10 and COST is less than 8.

FIGURE 3-16
Use of the AND logical
operator

Method 1: Using the AND logical operator.

```
200   IF NOT MARGIN > 10 AND COST < 8 THEN READ SELLING.PRICE
210
```

Method 2: Using nested IF statements.

```
200   IF MARGIN > 10
          THEN IF COST < 8
                 THEN READ SELLING.PRICE
210
```

In Method 1 of Figure 3-16, if MARGIN is greater than 10 and COST is less than 8, the READ statement assigns a value to SELLING.PRICE before control passes to line 210. If either one of the conditions is false, then the compound condition is false, and control passes to line 210 without a value being read for SELLING.PRICE. Although both methods are equivalent, Method 1 is more efficient, more compact, and more straightforward than Method 2.

Like a single condition, a compound condition can be only true or false. To determine the truth value of the compound condition, the computer must evaluate and assign a truth value to each individual condition. Then the truth value is determined for the compound condition.

For example, if A equals 4 and C$ equals "X", the computer evaluates the following compound condition in the manner shown:

```
300 IF A = 3 AND C$ = "X" THEN LET F = F + 1
        1. false        2. true
                3. false
```

The computer first determines the truth value for each condition, then concludes that the compound condition is false because of the AND operator.

The OR Logical Operator

The OR logical operator requires that only one of the two conditions be true for the compound condition to be true. If both conditions are true, the compound condition is also true. Likewise, if both conditions are false, the compound condition is false. The use of the OR operator is illustrated in Figure 3-17.

Method 1: Using the OR logical operator.
```
400   IF CODE$ = "A" OR MARITAL.STATUS$ = "M"
          THEN LET CNT = CNT + 1
410
```

Method 2: Using two IF statements.
```
400   IF CODE$ = "A" THEN LET CNT = CNT + 1 : GOTO 420
410   IF MARITAL.STATUS$ = "M" THEN LET CNT = CNT + 1
420
```

FIGURE 3-17   Use of the OR logical operator

In Method 1 of Figure 3-17, if either CODE$ equals the value A or MARTIAL.STATUS$ equals the value M, the THEN clause is executed and CNT is incremented by 1. If both conditions are true, the THEN clause is also executed. If both conditions are false, the THEN clause is bypassed, and control passes to line 410. Method 2 employs two IF statements to resolve the same If-Then-Else structure. Again, both methods are equivalent, but, Method 1 is easier to read and understand than Method 2.

As with the logical operator AND, the truth values of the individual conditions in the IF statement are first determined, then the truth values for the conditions containing the logical operator OR are evaluated. For example, if F equals 4 and H equals 5, the following condition is true:

```
500 IF F = 3 OR H = 5 THEN PRINT "Yes"
        1. false   2. true
            3. true
```

Combining Logical Operators

Logical operators can be combined in a decision statement to form a compound condition. The formation of compound statements that involve more than one type of logical operator can create problems unless you fully understand the order in which the computer evaluates the entire condition. Unless parentheses dictate otherwise, reading from left to right, conditions containing arithmetic operators are evaluated first; then those containing relational operators; then those containing NOT operators; then those containing AND operators; then those containing OR operators. Refer to the last page of the Reference Card at the back of this book for a summary listing of the order of both arithmetic and logical operators.

For the following compound condition, assume that D = 3, P = 5, R = 3, T = 5, S = 6, and Y = 3:

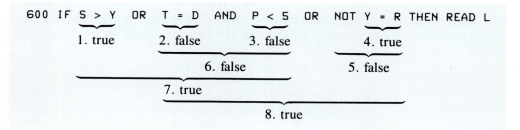

The Use of Parentheses in Compound Conditions

Parentheses may be used to change the order of precedence. When there are parentheses in a compound condition, the computer evaluates that part of the compound condition within the parentheses first, then continues to evaluate the remaining compound condition according to the order of logical operations. For example, suppose variable J has a value of 2, and E has a value of 6. Consider the following compound condition:

```
700 IF J = 7  AND E > 5  OR  J <> 0 THEN LET CNT = CNT + 1
        1. false     2. true     3. true
            4. false
                    5. true
```

Following the order of logical operations, the compound condition yields a truth value of true. If parentheses surround the last two conditions, then the OR operator is evaluated before the AND condition, and the compound condition yields a truth value of false, as shown:

```
800 IF J = 7  AND (E > 5  OR  J <> 0) THEN LET CNT = CNT + 1
       4. false      1. true     2. true
                         3. true
              5. false
```

Parentheses may be used freely when the evaluation of a compound condition is in doubt. For example, if you want to evaluate the compound condition

```
900 IF C > D AND S = 4 OR X < Y AND T = 5 THEN READ F
```

you can incorporate it into a decision statement as it stands. You can also write in the following way:

```
950 IF (C > D AND S = 4) OR (X < Y AND T = 5) THEN READ F
```

and feel more certain of the outcome of the decision statement.

THE ON-GOTO STATEMENT

The ON-GOTO statement is used to implement the case structure. Figure 3-18 illustrates the implementation of a case structure, which determines a letter grade (LETTER.GRADE$) from a grade point average (GPA) using the following grading scale:

GRADE POINT AVERAGE	LETTER GRADE
$90 \leq GPA \leq 100$	A
$80 \leq GPA < 90$	B
$70 \leq GPA < 80$	C
$60 \leq GPA < 70$	D
$0 \leq GPA < 60$	F
$GPA < 0$	Error

For example, if your GPA is 89.6, your letter grade is a B.

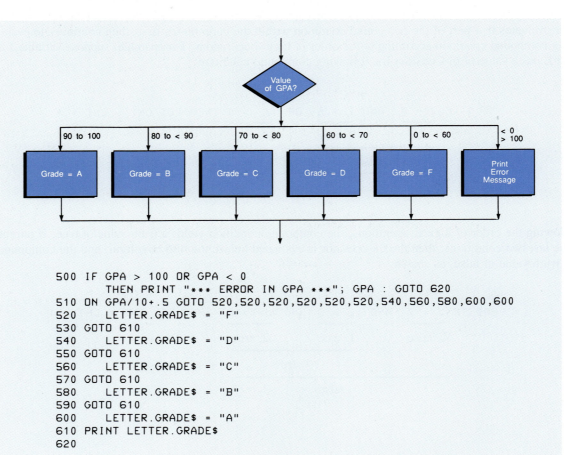

```
500 IF GPA > 100 OR GPA < 0
        THEN PRINT "*** ERROR IN GPA ***"; GPA : GOTO 620
510 ON GPA/10+.5 GOTO 520,520,520,520,520,520,540,560,580,600,600
520     LETTER.GRADE$ = "F"
530 GOTO 610
540     LETTER.GRADE$ = "D"
550 GOTO 610
560     LETTER.GRADE$ = "C"
570 GOTO 610
580     LETTER.GRADE$ = "B"
590 GOTO 610
600     LETTER.GRADE$ = "A"
610 PRINT LETTER.GRADE$
620
```

FIGURE 3-18 Implementation of a case structure

The ON-GOTO statement in line 510 of Figure 3-18 implements the grading scale. When the computer executes line 510, control transfers to one of the routines that are represented by the line numbers in the list following the keyword GOTO. If the rounded value of the condition (GPA/10 + .5) is 1, control transfers to the first line number in the list; if its 2, then control transfers to the second line number; and so on.

When the condition is evaluated, BASIC rounds it to the nearest integer. For example, if GPA is equal to 74, then GPA/10 + .5 equals 7.9. BASIC rounds 7.9 to 8 and control transfers to the eighth line number in the list (line 560). In line 560, LETTER.GRADE\$ is set equal to the value C. Line 570 transfers control to line 610 which prints the letter grade.

Figure 3-19 illustrates several GPA values and the corresponding line numbers to which control transfers due to line 510.

GPA	CONDITION GPA/10 + .5	ROUNDED TO INTEGER	CONTROL TRANSFERS TO	VALUE OF LETTER.GRADE\$
0	.5	1	520	F
9	1.4	1	520	F
39	4.4	4	520	F
59.99	6.499	6	520	F
65	7.0	7	540	D
70	7.5	8	560	C
89.99	9.499	9	580	B
91	9.6	10	600	A
100	10.5	11	600	A

FIGURE 3-19 Examples of transferring control to line numbers in the ON-GOTO statement in Figure 3-18 on the basis of different GPAs

In a BASIC program you should never permit the value of the condition in an ON-GOTO statement to be negative or zero. Furthermore, the value of the condition should not exceed the total number of line numbers in the list. Thus, in Figure 3-18, the IF statement (line 500) filters out GPA values that exceed 100 or are less than zero. The general form of the ON-GO statement is shown in Figure 3-20.

ON numeric expression GOTO lineno$_1$, lineno$_2$, ..., lineno$_n$

where the rounded integer value of **numeric expression** determines the line number to branch to

FIGURE 3-20 The general form of the ON-GOTO statement

TRY IT YOURSELF EXERCISES

1. Determine the value of AMT that will cause the condition in the following IF statements to be true:
   a. 100 IF Amt > 8 OR AMT = 3 THEN LET Z = Z / 10
   b. 200 IF AMT + 10 >= 7 AND NOT AMT < 0 THEN PRINT SALES.PRICE

2. Construct partial programs for each of these structures.

   a. 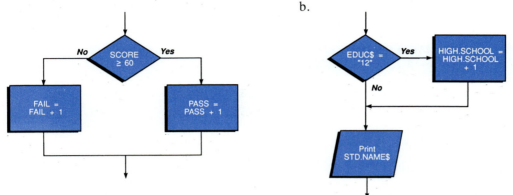 b.

3. Construct partial programs for each of these logic structures.

   a. 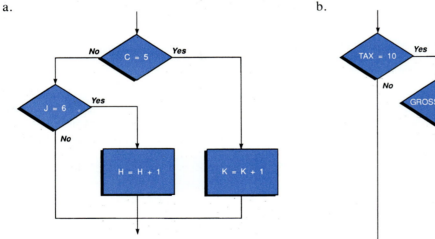 b.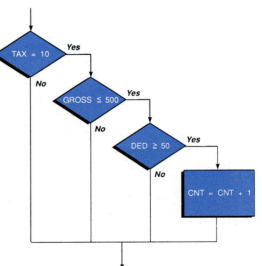

4. What is displayed if the following program is executed?

```
100 ' Exercise 4
110 READ I
120 WHILE I <> -99
130    IF I < 1 OR I > 4 THEN PRINT "*** ERROR ***"; I : GOTO 220
140    ON I GOTO 150, 170, 190, 210
150       PRINT I, "Case 1"
160    GOTO 220
170       PRINT I, "Case 2"
180    GOTO 220
190       PRINT I, "Case 3"
200    GOTO 220
210       PRINT I, "Case 4"
220    READ I
230 WEND
240 DATA 1, 4, 6, 2, 3, 0, -99
250 END
```

5. Given the following:

   EMP.NUM = 500
   SALARY = $700
   JOB.CODE$ = "1"
   TAX = $60
   INSURANCE.DED = $40

   Determine the truth value of these compound conditions:

   a. EMP.NUM < 400 OR JOB.CODE$ = "1"
   b. SALARY = 700 AND TAX = 50
   c. SALARY - TAX = 640 AND JOB.CODE$ = "1"
   d. TAX + INSURANCE.DED = SALARY - 500 OR JOB.CODE$ = "0"
   e. NOT JOB.CODE$ < "0"
   f. NOT (JOB.CODE$ = "1" OR TAX = 60)
   g. SALARY < 300 AND INSURANCE.DED < 50 OR JOB.CODE$ = "1"
   h. SALARY < 300 AND (INSURANCE.DED < 50 OR JOB.CODE$ = "1")
   i. NOT (NOT JOB.CODE$ = "1")

6. Given the following:

   $T = 0, V = 4, B = 7, Y = 8,$ and $X = 3$

   Determine the action taken for each of these statements:

   a. 300 IF T > 0 THEN READ A
   b. 400 IF B = 4 OR T > 7
              THEN IF X > 1 THEN READ A
   c. 500 IF X = 3 OR T > 2
              THEN IF Y > 7 THEN READ A
   d. 600 IF X + 2 < 5
              THEN IF B < V + X THEN READ A

7. Write a program that determines the number of negative values (NEGATIVE), number of zero values (ZERO) and number of positive values (POSITIVE) in the following data set: 4, 2, 3, –9, 0, 0, –4, –6, –8, 3, 2, 0, 0, 8, –3, 4. Use the –999999 to test for the end-of-file.

8. The values of three variables NUM1, NUM2, and NUM3 are positive and not equal to each other. Using IF statements, determine which has the smallest value and assign this value to LITTLE.

9. The IOU National Bank computes its monthly service charge on checking accounts by adding $0.50 to a value computed from the following:

   $0.21 per check for the first ten checks
   $0.19 per check for the next ten checks
   $0.17 per check for the next additional ten checks
   $0.15 per check for the remaining checks

   Write a partial program that includes an ON-GOTO statement and a PRINT statement to display the account number (ACCOUNT), the number of checks cashed (CHECKS), and the computed monthly charge (CHARGE).

STUDENT ASSIGNMENTS

STUDENT ASSIGNMENT 1: Student Registration Report

Instructions: Design and code a BASIC program to process the data shown under INPUT. Generate the student registration report shown under OUTPUT. A student with less than 12 hours is defined as part-time. The registration fee is determined from the following:

Credits Hours	Fee
Less than 12	$400.00
12 or more	$400.00 plus $30.00 per credit hour in excess of 11 hours

As part of the end-of-job routine, print the total number of part-time students, full-time students, students, and fees.

INPUT: Use the following sample data:

STUDENT NAME	CREDIT HOURS
Joe Franks	14
Ed Crane	9
Susan Lewis	18
Fred Smith	12
Jack North	10
Nikole Hiegh	17
EOF	0

OUTPUT: The following results are printed:

```
              Student Registration

Student      Credit
Name         Hours        Fee    Status

Joe Franks     14       490.00   Full-Time
Ed Crane        9       400.00   Part-Time
Susan Lewis    18       610.00   Full-Time
Fred Smith     12       430.00   Full-Time
Jack North     10       400.00   Part-Time
Nikole Hiegh   17       580.00   Full-Time

Total Part-Time ----->       2
Total Full-Time ----->       4
Total Students ------>       6
Total Fees ---------->  $2,910.00

End of Report
```

STUDENT ASSIGNMENT 2: Employee Salary Increase Report

Instructions: Design and code a BASIC program to process the data shown under INPUT. Use IF statements with compound conditions to display on the screen the employee salary increase report shown under OUTPUT.

Determine the employee salary increase from the following:

1. All employees get a 4% salary increase
2. Employees with more than three annual merits and 10 or more years of service get an additional 2.5% salary increase
3. Employees with four or more annual merits and less than 10 years of service get an additional 1.5% salary increase

INPUT: Use the following sample data. Make sure you enclose the employee names within quotation marks, since each name includes a comma.

EMPLOYEE NAME	ANNUAL MERITS	SERVICE	CURRENT SALARY
Babjack, Bill	9	3	$19,500
Knopf, Louis	0	19	29,200
Taylor, Jane	8	12	26,000
Droopey, Joe	8	4	28,000
Lane, Lyn	2	9	19,800
Lis, Frank	6	1	21,000
Lopez, Hector	10	1	15,000
Braion, Jim	8	19	26,500
EOF	0	0	0

OUTPUT: The following results are displayed:

```
            Employee Salary Increase Report

Employee      Annual     Current                    New
Name          Merits     Salary         Raise       Salary

Babjack, Bill    9       19,500.00      1,116.38    20,616.38
Knopf, Louis     0       29,200.00      1,168.00    30,368.00
Taylor, Jane     8       26,000.00      1,742.00    27,742.00
Droopey, Joe     8       28,000.00      1,596.00    29,596.00
Lane, Lyn        2       19,800.00        801.90    20,601.90
Lis, Frank       6       21,000.00      1,186.50    22,186.50
Lopez, Hector   10       15,000.00        862.50    15,862.50
Braion, Jim      8       26,500.00      1,775.50    28,275.50
                         -----------    --------    -----------
                        185,000.00     10,248.78   195,248.78

Total Employees ------------>       8
Average Employee Raise ------>  $1,281.10

End of Report
```

STUDENT ASSIGNMENT 3: Computer Usage Report

Instructions: Design and code a BASIC program to process the data shown under INPUT and print the report shown under OUTPUT. Use the ON-GOTO statement to determine the computer charges. At the end-of-job, print the total customers, total hours in decimal, and the total charges. The monthly charges can be determined from the following:

1. $165.00 for less than one hour of usage
2. $240.00 for usage greater than or equal to one hour and less than two hours
3. $300.00 for usage greater than or equal to two hours and less than three hours
4. $330.00 for usage greater than or equal to three hours and less than four hours
5. $375.00 for usage greater than or equal to four hours and less than five hours
6. $1.25 per minute if the usage is greater than or equal to five hours

INPUT: Use the following sample data:

CUSTOMER NAME	HOURS	MINUTES
Acme Inc.	0	20
Hitek	2	50
Floline	5	10
Niki's Food	1	14
Amanda Inc.	6	22
EOF	0	0

OUTPUT: The following results are printed:

```
                Computer Usage Report

    Customer
    Name          Hours       Minutes      Charges

    Acme Inc.        0            20        165.00
    Hitek            2            50        300.00
    Floline          5            10        387.50
    Niki's Food      1            14        240.00
    Amanda Inc.      6            22        477.50

    Total Customers ------->          5
    Total Hours     ----------->     15.93
    Total Charges   --------->  $1,570.00

    End of Report
```

PROJECT

MICROSOFT BASIC

Interactive Programming, For Loops, and an Introduction to the Top-Down Approach

OBJECTIVES

You will have mastered the material in this project when you can:

◆ State the purpose of the INPUT statement

◆ State the purpose of the BEEP statement

◆ State the purpose of the LOCATE statement

◆ Discuss data validation techniques

◆ Distinguish the difference between Do-While and Do-Until loops

◆ State the purposes of the FOR and NEXT statements

◆ List the parameters in a FOR statement

◆ Describe the top-down (modular) approach

◆ State the purposes of the GOSUB and RETURN statements

◆ Describe what a top-down chart shows and how it differs from a program flowchart

◆ Describe what is meant by nested GOSUBs

One of the major tasks of any program is to integrate the data that is to be processed into the program. In the first three projects, we used the READ and DATA statements to integrate the data into the program. This project introduces you to another method of data integration through the use of the INPUT statement. The INPUT statement is different than the READ and DATA statements, because with the INPUT statement the data is entered *during* execution rather than as *part of the program*.

A second topic covered in this project is alternative methods for implementing loops in BASIC. Through the first three projects, we have consistently created loops using the WHILE and WEND statements. In this project we discuss the creation of loops using the FOR and NEXT statements. The FOR and NEXT statements allow you to more efficiently establish counter-controlled loops. A **counter-controlled loop** is one that exits the loop when a counter has reached a specified number.

Finally, this project presents the top-down approach to solving problems. The top-down approach is a useful methodology for solving large and complex problems. This approach breaks the problem into smaller parts and allows you to solve each part independent of the others.

THE INPUT STATEMENT

◆ The INPUT statement causes a program to temporarily halt execution and accept data through the keyboard as shown on the next page in Figure 4-1. After the user enters the required data (1.25 in Figure 4-1) through the keyboard, the program continues to execute.

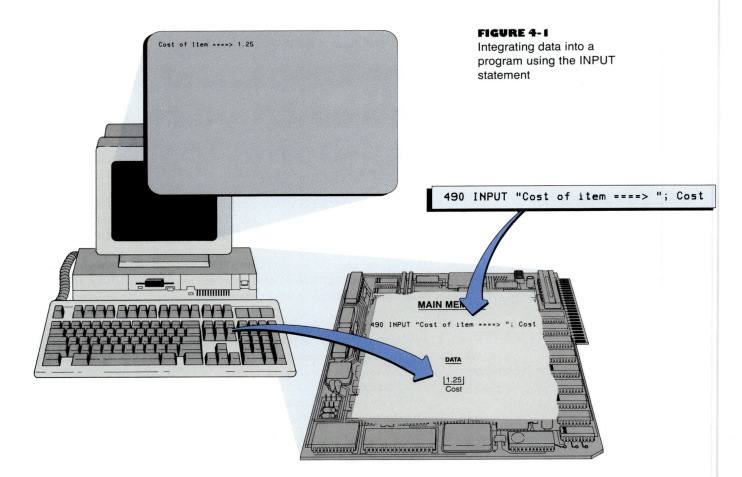

FIGURE 4-1
Integrating data into a program using the INPUT statement

The INPUT statement has two general forms, shown in Figure 4-2. With the first general form, the keyword INPUT is immediately followed by one or more variables separated by commas. When executed, this first form displays a question mark on the screen to indicate that it is waiting for the user to enter data.

The second general form of the INPUT statement shows that the programmer may enter a **prompt message** to inform the user of the required data. In this second and most often used form, the keyword INPUT is followed by the prompt message in quotation marks, a comma or semicolon after the prompt message, and a list of variables separated by commas. A semicolon after a prompt message tells the computer to display a question mark immediately after the prompt message. A comma instructs the computer not to display the question mark. Although this statement may include more than one variable, most programmers place one variable per INPUT statement.

No Prompt Message

INPUT variable, …, variable

Prompt Message

INPUT "prompt message", variable, …, variable

FIGURE 4-2   The general forms of the INPUT statement

Figure 4-3 illustrates several examples of INPUT statements.

EXAMPLE	INPUT STATEMENT	DATA ENTERED THROUGH KEYBOARD
1	500 INPUT AMOUNT, COST	125.56, 75
2	510 INPUT CUS.NAME$, AGE, DEDUCTION	Joe Dac, 57, 25
3	520 INPUT "Discount =====>", DISC	.25
4	530 INPUT "What is your name"; USER.NAME$	Marci Jean
5	540 PRINT "Do you want to continue?" 550 INPUT "Enter Y for Yes, else N", CONTROL$	Y

FIGURE 4-3 Examples of the INPUT statement

Examples 1 and 2 in Figure 4-3 show that it is not necessary to include a prompt message. When either INPUT statement is executed, a question mark displays on the screen. Examples 3 through 5 include prompt messages. In Example 3, the prompt message

```
Discount =====>
```

displays on the screen at the location of the cursor. Following the display of the prompt, the computer halts execution until the user enters the data (.25) and presses the Enter key.

In Example 4 of Figure 4-3, the following prompt displays:

```
What is your name?
```

Because we ended the prompt message with a semicolon, the computer displays the question mark after the prompt. Example 5 shows how you can utilize the PRINT statement along with the INPUT statement to display prompt messages made up of more than one line.

THE BEEP AND LOCATE STATEMENTS

◆ Two BASIC statements that are often used in tandem with the INPUT statement are the BEEP and LOCATE statements.

The BEEP Statement

When executed, the BEEP statement causes the computer's speaker to beep for a fraction of a second. Several BEEP statements in a row cause the computer to beep for a longer duration. The following line causes the computer to beep for approximately one second:

```
510 BEEP : BEEP : BEEP : BEEP
```

Notice the colons between the BEEP statements. In BASIC, the colon allows you to place more than one statement per line. The BEEP statement is often used to alert the user that there is a problem with the program or data.

The LOCATE Statement

BASIC defines the output screen as having 25 rows and 80 columns. The LOCATE statement can be used to position the cursor precisely on any one of the two thousand display positions on the screen. For example, the following line causes the computer to move the cursor to row 4, column 15:

```
520 LOCATE 4, 15
```

It makes no difference whether the cursor is above or below row 4 or to the right or left of column 15. The general form of the LOCATE statement is shown in Figure 4-4.

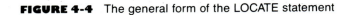

LOCATE row, column

FIGURE 4-4   The general form of the LOCATE statement

When executed, the partial program in Figure 4-5 displays the prompt message in the INPUT statement in row 6, column 12.

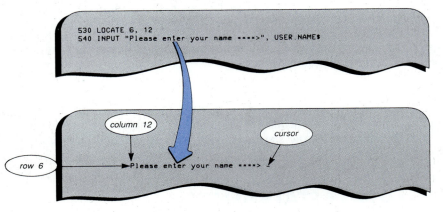

```
530 LOCATE 6, 12
540 INPUT "Please enter your name ====>", USER.NAMES
```

column 12

cursor

row 6 ──→ ►Please enter your name ====>

FIGURE 4-5   Use of the LOCATE statement to position the cursor

EDITING DATA ENTERED THROUGH THE KEYBOARD

◆ In most interactive applications it is required that you check the incoming data to be sure that it is reasonable. A **reasonableness check** ensures that the data is legitimate, that is, the data is within a range of acceptable values. If the data is not validated before being used, then the computer can very well generate incorrect information.

The partial program in Figure 4-6 requests that the user enter a value for the variable ITEM.COST. Assume that the program specifications state that the value of ITEM.COST must be greater than zero and less than 1,000.00.

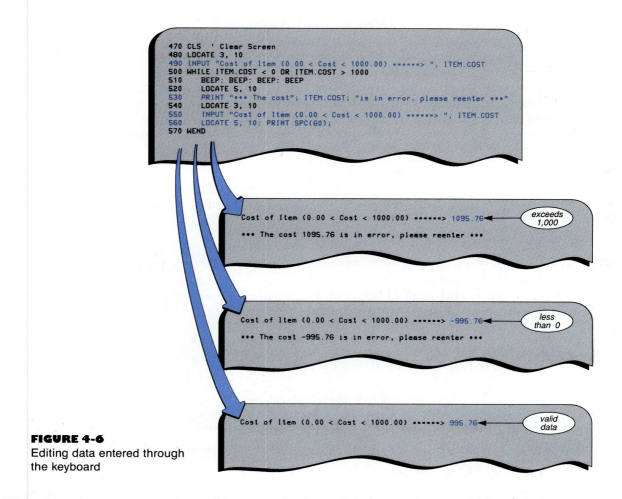

```
470 CLS  ' Clear Screen
480 LOCATE 3, 10
490 INPUT "Cost of Item (0.00 < Cost < 1000.00) ••••••> ", ITEM.COST
500 WHILE ITEM.COST < 0 OR ITEM.COST > 1000
510    BEEP: BEEP: BEEP: BEEP
520    LOCATE 5, 10
530    PRINT "••• The cost"; ITEM.COST; "is in error, please reenter •••"
540    LOCATE 3, 10
550    INPUT "Cost of Item (0.00 < Cost < 1000.00) ••••••> ", ITEM.COST
560    LOCATE 5, 10: PRINT SPC(60);
570 WEND
```

```
Cost of Item (0.00 < Cost < 1000.00) ••••••> 1095.76       exceeds
                                                            1,000
••• The cost 1095.76 is in error, please reenter •••
```

```
Cost of Item (0.00 < Cost < 1000.00) ••••••> -995.76       less
                                                           than 0
••• The cost -995.76 is in error, please reenter •••
```

```
Cost of Item (0.00 < Cost < 1000.00) ••••••> 995.76        valid
                                                           data
```

FIGURE 4-6
Editing data entered through
the keyboard

When the computer executes the partial program in Figure 4-6, the CLS statement in line 470 clears the output screen. Line 480 moves the cursor to column 10 in row 3. The INPUT statement in line 490 displays the prompt message and halts execution of the program. After the user enters the value 1095.76 and presses the Enter key, the WHILE statement in line 500 tests the value of ITEM.COST. Since it is greater than 1,000.00, control enters the loop. Line 510 causes the computer speaker to beep for a second. Due to lines 520 and 530, the computer displays an error message beginning at column 10 in row 5.

Lines 540 and 550 again cause the prompt message to display beginning at column 10 in row 3. After the user enters -995.76, the error message in row 5 is erased by the SPC function in the PRINT statement in line 560. The SPC function displays as many spaces as indicated in the parentheses. Thus, SPC(60) displays 60 spaces and in doing so erases the error message in row 5. Since -995.76 is still outside the limits, the computer reexecutes the loop and displays the error message due to line 530. Finally, when the user enters 995.76, the computer exits the loop and continues execution at the line following the WEND statement in line 570.

Data validation is an important part of the programming process. It should be apparent that the information produced by a computer is only as accurate as the data it processes. The term **GIGO** (Garbage In—Garbage Out, pronounced GEE-GOH) is used to describe the generation of inaccurate information from the input of invalid data. Data validation should be incorporated into all programs, especially when the INPUT statement is used.

SAMPLE PROGRAM 4 — ITEM COST REPORT

◆   The sample program in this project illustrates the preparation of an item cost table that contains the cost of one to ten items. The program begins by asking the user to enter the cost of an item. The cost must be greater than zero and less than 1,000.00. After validating the entry, the sample program displays the cost table. Once the table displays, the user is asked if another table should be prepared. The user must enter a Y for yes or an N for no.

If the user enters the letter Y, the loop is executed again and the user is asked to enter the cost of the next item. If the user enters the letter N, the program displays an end-of-job message followed by termination of execution. Figure 4-7 shows the desired output results for Sample Program 4.

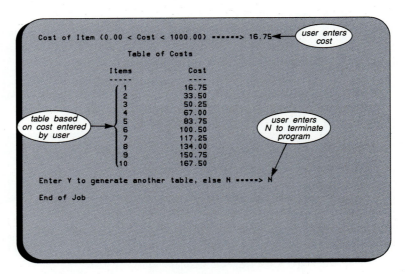

FIGURE 4-7   The desired output results for Sample Program 4

Program Flowchart

The flowchart for Sample Program 4 which produces the item cost table for one to ten items is illustrated in Figure 4-8. At the top of the flowchart, the variable representing the maximum number of items is initialized, the table format is assigned to string variables, the twenty-fifth line is turned off, and CONTROL$ is set equal to the value Y.

Control then enters the loop. Notice that this is the first time in these projects that a decision symbol is not at the top of the loop. In this flowchart, the decision to terminate the loop is at the bottom. Loops that have the decision to terminate at the top are called Do-While loops. Loops that have the decision to terminate at the bottom are called Do-Until loops.

Within the major loop, the output screen is cleared and the user is requested to enter the cost of an item. Next, the cost is validated, the table headings are displayed, and a counter is initialized to one. The table is then generated by a looping process that continues while the counter is less than or equal to the table limit. After the table displays, the user is asked if another table is desired. The decision symbol at the bottom of the Do-Until loop determines whether to continue or terminate processing on the basis of the value (Y or N) entered by the user.

Before we can code the logic shown in Figure 4-8 we need to discuss the FOR and NEXT statements.

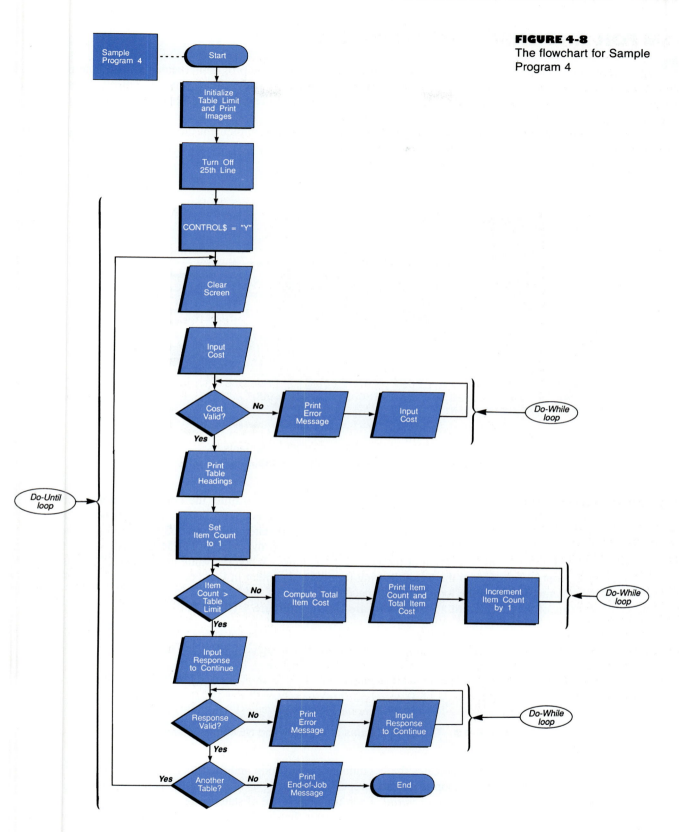

FIGURE 4-8
The flowchart for Sample
Program 4

THE FOR AND NEXT STATEMENTS

◆   The FOR and NEXT statements make it possible to execute a section of a program repeatedly, with automatic changes in the value of a variable between repetitions. Whenever you have to develop a counter-controlled loop (a loop that is to be executed a specific number of times based on a counter), you can use the FOR and NEXT statements to develop it. We call such a loop a **For loop**.

Figure 4-9 illustrates how the FOR and NEXT statements can be used to implement the loop that generates the cost table described in the flowchart for Sample Program 4.

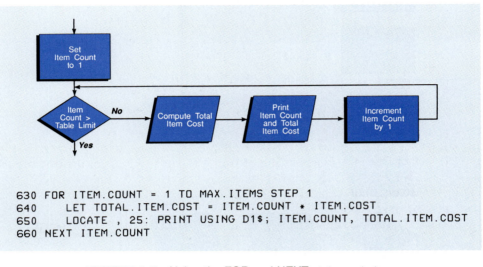

```
630 FOR ITEM.COUNT = 1 TO MAX.ITEMS STEP 1
640    LET TOTAL.ITEM.COST = ITEM.COUNT * ITEM.COST
650    LOCATE , 25: PRINT USING D1$; ITEM.COUNT, TOTAL.ITEM.COST
660 NEXT ITEM.COUNT
```

FIGURE 4-9   Using the FOR and NEXT statements to implement the loop that generates the cost table

When the FOR statement in line 630 of Figure 4-9 is executed for the first time, the For loop becomes active and the variable ITEM.COUNT is set equal to one. The statements within the For loop, in this case lines 640 and 650, are executed. The NEXT statement in line 660 returns control to the FOR statement in line 630, where the value of ITEM.COUNT is incremented by 1, which follows the keyword STEP. If the value of ITEM.COUNT is less than or equal to MAX.ITEMS (table limit), execution of the For loop continues. When the value of ITEM.COUNT is greater than MAX.ITEMS, control transfers to the line following the NEXT statement in line 660. As with other loops, notice that we indent the statements within the loop by three spaces.

The general forms of the FOR and NEXT statements are shown in Figure 4-10.

FOR loop-variable = initial TO limit STEP increment

   [range of statements]

NEXT loop-variable

FIGURE 4-10   The general forms of the FOR and NEXT statements

In Figure 4-10, the FOR statement indicates the beginning of a For loop and the NEXT statement indicates the end. The range of statements within the For loop is executed repeatedly as long as *loop-variable* is not greater than *limit*. *Loop-variable* is initially assigned the value of *initial*. Each time the range of statements is executed, *loop-variable* is increased by the value of *increment*. When *loop-variable* is greater than *limit*, control passes to the line following the corresponding NEXT statement.

If *increment* is negative, the test to terminate the For loop is reversed. The value of *loop-variable* is decremented each time through the For loop, and the For loop is executed while *loop-variable* is greater than or equal to *limit*. If the keyword STEP is not included in a FOR statement, then the increment value is automatically set to one.

Figure 4-11 illustrates several valid FOR statements.

EXAMPLE	FOR STATEMENT
1	FOR COUNT = 1 TO 100 STEP 1
2	FOR X = 5 TO Y STEP 3
3	FOR AMOUNT = 1.25 TO 7.35 STEP .05
4	FOR TAX = A TO B STEP C
5	FOR S = 0 TO -35 STEP -3
6	FOR X = 1 TO 10

FIGURE 4-11   Examples of valid FOR statements

In Example 1 of Figure 4-11, the For loop is executed 100 times. Example 2 points out that the initial and increment values can be values other than one. Example 3 initializes AMOUNT to 1.25 for the first pass. Thereafter, the value .05 is added to AMOUNT each time the range of statements is executed. Hence, AMOUNT takes on the values 1.25, 1.30, 1.35, 1.40, and so on, until AMOUNT exceeds 7.35.

Example 4 shows that the initial, limit, and increment values can be variables. Example 5 includes a negative increment (-3). Thus, the test is reversed and S must be less than -35 before the For loop terminates. Finally, Example 6 illustrates a FOR statement without the keyword STEP. In this case, the increment value is automatically set to one.

The BASIC Program

The program in Figure 4-12 corresponds to the program flowchart on page MB67 in Figure 4-8.

FIGURE 4-12
Sample Program 4

```
100 ' ****************************************************************
110 ' * Sample Program 4                        September 15, 1994  *
120 ' * Item Cost Report                                            *
130 ' * J. S. Quasney                                               *
140 ' *                                                             *
150 ' * This program displays a table of costs of 1 to 10 items. *
160 ' * The user enters the cost per item and the program          *
170 ' * displays the table of costs.                               *
180 ' *    The cost per item entered by the user is validated      *
190 ' * (greater than zero and less than 1000.00).  After the      *
200 ' * table is displayed the user is asked if another table      *
210 ' * should be generated.                                       *
220 ' *    This activity continues until the user indicates        *
230 ' * that no more tables are to be generated.                   *
240 ' *                                                             *
250 ' * Variables:  ITEM.COST       -- Cost of item                *
260 ' *             ITEM.COUNT      -- Item count                  *
270 ' *             MAX.ITEMS       --'Maximum number of items     *
280 ' *                                in table                    *
290 ' *             TOTAL.ITEM.COST -- Cost of items               *
300 ' *             CONTROL$        -- Response to continue        *
310 ' *             H1$, H2$, H3$, D1$, T1$ -- Print images        *
320 ' ****************************************************************
330 '
```

(continued)

```
340 ' ********************** Initialization **********************
350 LET MAX.ITEMS = 10
360 LET H1$ = "     Table of Costs"
370 LET H2$ = "Items           Cost"
380 LET H3$ = "-----          ----"
390 LET D1$ = "  ##        ##,###.##"
400 LET T1$ = "End of Job"
410 KEY OFF  ' Turn off 25th line on screen
420 '
430 ' ******************** Create Cost Table **********************
440 LET CONTROL$ = "Y"
450 WHILE CONTROL$ = "Y"
460    ' ***************** Accept Cost of Item *******************
470    CLS  ' Clear Screen
480    LOCATE 3, 10
490    INPUT "Cost of Item (0.00 < Cost < 1000.00) ======> ", ITEM.COST
500    WHILE ITEM.COST < 0 OR ITEM.COST > 1000
510       BEEP: BEEP: BEEP: BEEP
520       LOCATE 5, 10
530       PRINT "*** The cost"; ITEM.COST; "is in error, please reenter ***"
540       LOCATE 3, 10
550       INPUT "Cost of Item (0.00 < Cost < 1000.00) ======> ", ITEM.COST
560       LOCATE 5, 10: PRINT SPC(60);
570    WEND
580    '
590    ' ***************** Create Table of Costs ******************
600    LOCATE 5, 25: PRINT H1$
610    LOCATE 7, 25: PRINT H2$
620    LOCATE 8, 25: PRINT H3$
630    FOR ITEM.COUNT = 1 TO MAX.ITEMS STEP 1
640       LET TOTAL.ITEM.COST = ITEM.COUNT * ITEM.COST
650       LOCATE , 25: PRINT USING D1$; ITEM.COUNT, TOTAL.ITEM.COST
660    NEXT ITEM.COUNT
670    '
680    ' ************* Accept Response to Continue ***************
690    LOCATE 20, 10
700    INPUT "Enter Y to generate another table, else N =====> ", CONTROL$
710    WHILE CONTROL$ <> "N" AND CONTROL$ <> "Y"
720       BEEP: BEEP: BEEP: BEEP
730       LOCATE 22, 10
740       PRINT "*** Response in error, please reenter ***"
750       LOCATE 20, 10
760       INPUT "Enter Y to generate another table, else N =====> ", CONTROL$
770       LOCATE 22, 10: PRINT SPC(50);
780    WEND
790    '
800 WEND
810 '
820 ' ************************* Wrap-Up **************************
830 LOCATE 22, 10
840 PRINT T1$
850 END
```

FIGURE 4-12   (continued)

Discussion of Sample Program 4

When Sample Program 4 is executed, the variables in lines 350 through 400 are initialized. Line 350 initializes MAX.ITEMS (table limit) to 10. Lines 360 through 400 define the table format. The variables are used later in the PRINT statements in lines 600 through 620, 650, and 840. Line 410 clears the twenty-fifth line on the screen. In this program, we separate the CLS and KEY OFF statements because the CLS statement (line 470) must be executed each time through the loop to clear the screen for the next set of data. The KEY OFF statement need only be executed once, at the beginning of the program.

The Do-Until loop in the flowchart in Figure 4-11 is established in the program by the LET statement in line 440, the WHILE statement in line 450, and the WEND statement in line 800. Line 440 assigns CONTROL$ the value Y, thus ensuring that the WHILE statement in line 450 will allow control to pass into the body of the loop on the first pass. The WEND statement in line 800 signals the end of the Do-Until loop.

Upon entering the Do-Until loop, the screen is cleared by line 470. Lines 480 through 570 accept and validate the cost of the item entered by the user. Lines 600 through 620 display the table title and column headings. Lines 630 through 660 compute and display the rows of the table. Notice in line 650 that the LOCATE statement does not include a row number. When the LOCATE statement is written in this fashion, it references the current row, which is one greater than the one referenced by the previously executed PRINT or PRINT USING statement. Hence, each time line 650 is executed in the For loop, the PRINT USING statement begins printing in column 25 of the next row. Notice in lines 600 through 620 and 650 that it is common practice to incorporate both the LOCATE and PRINT statements on the same line. Of course, it is important that you separate the two statements with the colon.

After the table is displayed on the screen, lines 690 through 780 accept and validate a response from the user that indicates whether the Do-Until loop should continue. In this case, only two values, Y and N, are acceptable (line 710). Once the user enters a Y or an N, the WEND statement in line 800 transfers control to the corresponding WHILE statement in line 450. If the user enters a Y, line 450 causes the computer to continue execution of the loop. If the user enters the value N, the condition in line 450 is false. Thus, control passes to line 830 and an end-of-job message displays followed by termination of execution of the program.

Figure 4-13 shows the display of Sample Program 4 when the value 579.46 is entered as the cost of an item. To better understand how the program in Figure 4-12 works, we suggest you take the place of the computer and step through the instructions beginning with line 340. With paper and pencil, keep track of all the variables and write down items displayed. When you come to the INPUT statement in line 490, enter 579.46. When you come to the INPUT statement in line 700, enter the letter N. See if you don't end up with the results shown in Figure 4-13.

```
Cost of Item (0.00 < Cost < 1000.00) ------> 579.46

             Table of Costs

         Items          Cost
         -----          ----
           1           579.46
           2         1,158.92
           3         1,738.38
           4         2,317.84
           5         2,897.30
           6         3,476.76
           7         4,056.22
           8         4,635.68
           9         5,215.14
          10         5,794.60

Enter Y to generate another table, else N ------> N

End of Job
```

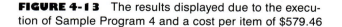

FIGURE 4-13 The results displayed due to the execution of Sample Program 4 and a cost per item of $579.46

AN INTRODUCTION TO THE TOP-DOWN APPROACH

◆ Top-down programming is a divide and conquer strategy used by programmers to solve large problems. The first step in top-down programming is to divide the task into smaller, more manageable subtasks through the use of a top-down chart. Figure 4-14 illustrates a top-down chart for the problem solved by Sample Program 4.

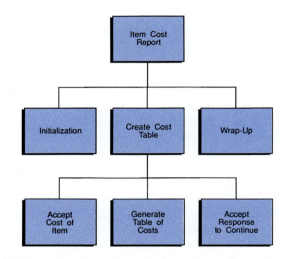

FIGURE 4-14 A top-down chart for the problem solved by Sample Program 4

A top-down chart differs from a program flowchart in that it does not show decision-making logic or flow of control. A program flowchart shows *how* to solve the problem. A top-down chart shows *what* has to be done.

A top-down chart is very similar to a company's organization chart where each lower level subtask carries out a function for its superior task. In Figure 4-14, the top box (Item Cost Report) represents the complete task. The next level of boxes (Initialization, Create Cost Table, and Wrap-Up) shows the subtasks that are required to solve the task of the top box. The lowest level of boxes (Accept Cost of Item, Generate Table of Costs, and Accept Response to Continue) indicates the subtasks required to create a table. Usually, a task is divided into lower level subtasks whenever it appears to be too complicated or lengthy to stand by itself.

Implementing the Top-Down Approach

Once the larger, more complex problem has been decomposed into smaller pieces, a solution to each subtask can be designed and coded. We call the group of statements that are associated with a single programming task a **subroutine**, or **module**.

The subroutines that formulate a program solution begin with a comment and end with a RETURN statement. Subroutines are *called* by their superior modules using the GOSUB statement. When a subroutine has completed its task, control returns to the superior module via a RETURN statement. The rules regarding a subroutine name are the same as for a variable name.

THE GOSUB AND RETURN STATEMENTS

◆   The GOSUB statement is used to call a subroutine. As shown in Figure 4-15, the keyword GOSUB is immediately followed by the line number of the subroutine to which control is transferred. Once control transfers, the instructions in the subroutine are executed.

FIGURE 4-15
The general form of the
GOSUB statement

GOSUB line-number

The RETURN statement (Figure 4-16) at the bottom of the subroutine returns control to the statement following the corresponding GOSUB in the superior module.

FIGURE 4-16
The general form of the
RETURN statement

RETURN

Consider the partial program shown on the next page in Figure 4-17 and the following important points regarding the implementation of the top-down approach:

- A subroutine does not have a unique *initial* statement to differentiate it from other subroutines or from the Main Module. To highlight the beginning of first-level subroutines, use a boxed-in remark before the first executable statement, as illustrated by lines 2000 to 2020 in Figure 4-17.
- The END statement is the last statement in the Main Module. Control returns to the BASICA prompt through this statement.
- Begin the prologue with line 1000 and each subsequent first-level subroutine with 2000, 3000, 4000, and so on. Begin lower-level subroutines called by the first-level subroutine beginning at 2000, with 2200, 2400, 2600, and so on. Don't concern yourself with consistent line numbering until your program is working properly. When you are ready to renumber your program, use the RENUM command. For example,

      RENUM 1000

  will renumber the entire program, beginning with line 1000 and using increments of 10. After renumbering the program, list the first 20 lines (LIST 1000-1200). Renumber the program again; only this time, renumber beginning with the subroutine that follows the Main Module. If the subroutine begins with line 1150, then the following command will renumber beginning at line 1150, with a starting line number of 2000 and with increments of 10:

      RENUM 2000, 1150

  List the next 20 lines, beginning with line 2000, and continue the process until the entire program has been renumbered as suggested.
- For purposes of readability, insert a comment line, using the apostrophe after each module, as shown in Figure 4-17, lines 1310 and 3100.
- With the GOSUB statement, you have the choice of referencing the first remark line or the first executable statement of the subroutine. In these projects we reference the first remark line of the subroutine, as illustrated in line 1270 of Figure 4-17. The GOSUB references line 2000, which is a remark line. When control transfers to a remark line, the computer automatically passes control to the first executable statement following the remark line.
- So that lower-level modules can be located easily for debugging purposes, they should be placed below the module that calls them and in the order in which they are called.

Consider the partial program shown on the next page in Figure 4-17 and the following important points regarding the implementation of the top-down approach:

A top-down version of Sample Program 4 is illustrated on pages MB75 and MB76 in Figure 4-18.

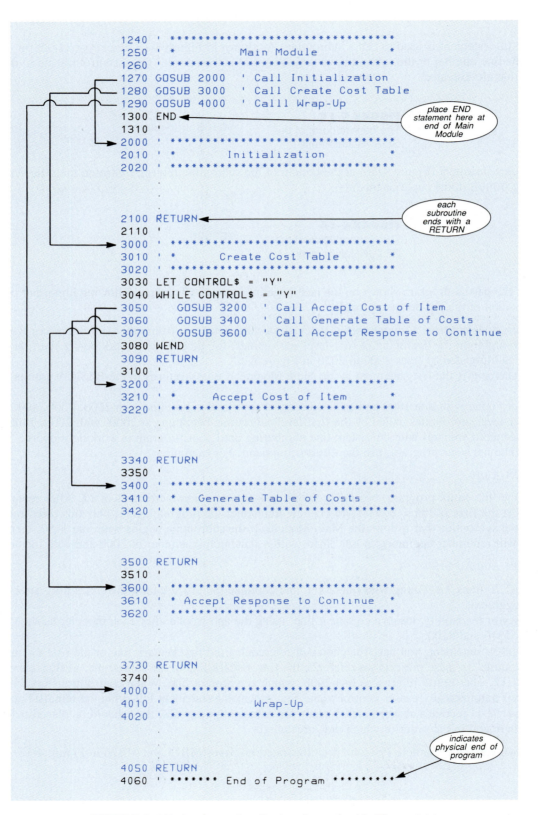

```
1240 ' *******************************
1250 ' *          Main Module          *
1260 ' *******************************
1270 GOSUB 2000   ' Call Initialization
1280 GOSUB 3000   ' Call Create Cost Table
1290 GOSUB 4000   ' Calll Wrap-Up
1300 END
1310 '
2000 ' *******************************
2010 ' *          Initialization          *
2020 ' *******************************
        .
        .
        .
2100 RETURN
2110 '
3000 ' *******************************
3010 ' *        Create Cost Table        *
3020 ' *******************************
3030 LET CONTROL$ = "Y"
3040 WHILE CONTROL$ = "Y"
3050     GOSUB 3200   ' Call Accept Cost of Item
3060     GOSUB 3400   ' Call Generate Table of Costs
3070     GOSUB 3600   ' Call Accept Response to Continue
3080 WEND
3090 RETURN
3100 '
3200 ' *******************************
3210 ' *        Accept Cost of Item        *
3220 ' *******************************
        .
        .
        .
3340 RETURN
3350 '
3400 ' *******************************
3410 ' *      Generate Table of Costs      *
3420 ' *******************************
        .
        .
        .
3500 RETURN
3510 '
3600 ' *******************************
3610 ' * Accept Response to Continue *
3620 ' *******************************
        .
        .
        .
3730 RETURN
3740 '
4000 ' *******************************
4010 ' *             Wrap-Up             *
4020 ' *******************************
        .
        .
        .
4050 RETURN
4060 ' ******* End of Program *********
```

place END statement here at end of Main Module

each subroutine ends with a RETURN

indicates physical end of program

FIGURE 4-17   Implementing the top-down chart in Figure 4-14

```
1000 ' ************************************************************
1010 ' *   Sample Program 4 Modified          September 15, 1994  *
1020 ' *   Item Cost Report                                       *
1030 ' *   J. S. Quasney                                          *
1040 ' *                                                          *
1050 ' *   This program displays a table of costs of 1 to 10 items. *
1060 ' *   The user enters the cost per item and the program      *
1070 ' *   generates the table of costs.                          *
1080 ' *        The cost per item entered by the user is validated *
1090 ' *   (greater than zero and less than 1000.00).  After the  *
1100 ' *   table is displayed the user is asked if another table  *
1110 ' *   should be generated.                                   *
1120 ' *        This activity continues until the user indicates  *
1130 ' *   that no more tables are to be generated.               *
1140 ' *                                                          *
1150 ' *   Variables:   ITEM.COST       -- Cost of item           *
1160 ' *               ITEM.COUNT       -- Item count             *
1170 ' *               MAX.ITEMS        -- Maximum number of item  *
1180 ' *                                  in table                *
1190 ' *               TOTAL.ITEM.COST  -- Cost of items           *
1200 ' *               CONTROL$         -- Response to continue    *
1210 ' *               H1$, H2$, H3$, D1$, T1$ -- Print images      *
1220 ' ************************************************************
1230 '
1240 ' ************************************************************
1250 ' *                       Main Module                        *
1260 ' ************************************************************
1270 GOSUB 2000   ' Call Initialization
1280 GOSUB 3000   ' Call Create Cost Table
1290 GOSUB 4000   ' Call Wrap-Up
1300 END
1310 '
2000 ' ************************************************************
2010 ' *                     Initialization                       *
2020 ' ************************************************************
2030 LET MAX.ITEMS = 10
2040 LET H1$ = "    Table of Costs"
2050 LET H2$ = "Items            Cost"
2060 LET H3$ = "-----            ----"
2070 LET D1$ = "  ##         ##,###.##"
2080 LET T1$ = "End of Job"
2090 KEY OFF   ' Turn off 25th line on screen
2100 RETURN
2110 '
3000 ' ************************************************************
3010 ' *                   Create Cost Table                      *
3020 ' ************************************************************
3030 LET CONTROL$ = "Y"
3040 WHILE CONTROL$ = "Y"
3050    GOSUB 3200  ' Call Accept Cost of Item
3060    GOSUB 3400  ' Call Generate Table of Costs
3070    GOSUB 3600  ' Call Accept Response to Continue
3080 WEND
3090 RETURN
3100 '
```

FIGURE 4-18 A top-down version of Sample Program 4   *(continued)*

```
3200 ' ***************************************************************
3210 ' *                   Accept Cost of Item                     *
3220 ' ***************************************************************
3230 CLS   ' Clear Screen
3240 LOCATE 3, 10
3250 INPUT "Cost of Item (0.00 < Cost < 1000.00) ======> ", ITEM.COST
3260 WHILE ITEM.COST < 0 OR ITEM.COST > 1000
3270    BEEP: BEEP: BEEP: BEEP
3280    LOCATE 5, 10
3290    PRINT "*** The cost"; ITEM.COST; "is in error, please reenter ***"
3300    LOCATE 3, 10
3310    INPUT "Cost of Item (0.00 < Cost < 1000.00) ======> ", ITEM.COST
3320    LOCATE 5, 10: PRINT SPC(60);
3330 WEND
3340 RETURN
3350 '
3400 ' ***************************************************************
3410 ' *                  Generate Table of Costs                  *
3420 ' ***************************************************************
3430 LOCATE 5, 25: PRINT H1$
3440 LOCATE 7, 25: PRINT H2$
3450 LOCATE 8, 25: PRINT H3$
3460 FOR ITEM.COUNT = 1 TO MAX.ITEMS STEP 1
3470    LET TOTAL.ITEM.COST = ITEM.COUNT * ITEM.COST
3480    LOCATE , 25: PRINT USING D1$; ITEM.COUNT, TOTAL.ITEM.COST
3490 NEXT ITEM.COUNT
3500 RETURN
3510 '
3600 ' ***************************************************************
3610 ' *                Accept Response to Continue                *
3620 ' ***************************************************************
3630 LOCATE 20, 10
3640 INPUT "Enter Y to generate another table, else N =====> ", CONTROL$
3650 WHILE CONTROL$ <> "N" AND CONTROL$ <> "Y"
3660    BEEP: BEEP: BEEP: BEEP
3670    LOCATE 22, 10
3680    PRINT "*** Response in error, please reenter ***"
3690    LOCATE 20, 10
3700    INPUT "Enter Y to generate another table, else N =====> ", CONTROL$
3710    LOCATE 22, 10: PRINT SPC(50);
3720 WEND
3730 RETURN
3740 '
4000 ' ***************************************************************
4010 ' *                          Wrap-Up                          *
4020 ' ***************************************************************
4030 LOCATE 22, 10
4040 PRINT T1$
4050 RETURN
4060 ' ******************** End of Program *********************
```

FIGURE 4-18   (continued)

Discussion of Sample Program 4 Modified

When the modified version of Sample Program 4 in Figure 4-18 executes, line 1270 in the Main Module transfers control to the Initialization module which begins at line 2000. After lines 2030 through 2090 are executed, the RETURN statement in line 2100 transfers control back to line 1280 in the Main Module. Next, line 1280 transfers control to the Create Cost Table module (lines 3000 through 3090). In this module, the Do-Until loop includes three GOSUB statements. Each time through this loop, a cost table such as the one in Figure 4-19 is generated.

When the user enters the letter N in response to the INPUT statement in line 3640, control passes back to line 3080. Since the condition in line 3040 is false, control passes to the RETURN statement in line 3090. Line 3090 returns control to line 1290. Next, line 1290 transfers control to the Wrap-Up module which begins at line 4000. After the end-of-job message is displayed, control returns to line 1300 in the Main Module and the program terminates execution.

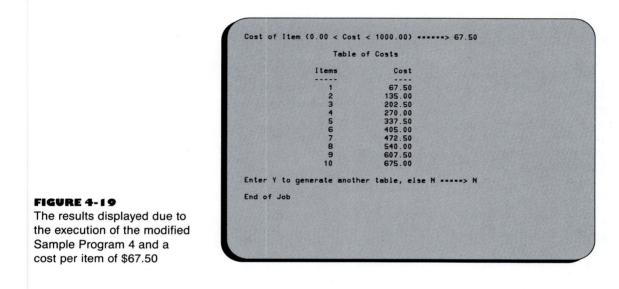

FIGURE 4-19
The results displayed due to the execution of the modified Sample Program 4 and a cost per item of $67.50

```
Cost of Item (0.00 < Cost < 1000.00) ======> 67.50

                    Table of Costs

            Items              Cost
            -----              ----
              1               67.50
              2              135.00
              3              202.50
              4              270.00
              5              337.50
              6              405.00
              7              472.50
              8              540.00
              9              607.50
             10              675.00

Enter Y to generate another table, else N ======> N

End of Job
```

TRY IT YOURSELF EXERCISES

1. What is displayed if each of the following programs are executed?
   a. X is assigned the value 2, and Y is assigned the value 4.

```
100 ' Exercise 1.a
110 INPUT "Enter values for X and Y ===> ", X, Y
120 SUM = X + Y
130 DIFF = Y - X
140 PROD = X * Y
150 QUOT = X / Y
160 PRINT SUM, DIFF
170 PRINT PROD, QUOT
180 END
```

b.

```
100 ' Exercise 1.b
110 COUNT = 0
120 GOSUB 210
130 PRINT COUNT
140 GOSUB 210
150 PRINT COUNT
160 GOSUB 210
170 PRINT COUNT
180 COUNT = COUNT - 3
190 PRINT COUNT
200 END
210 ' ***Increment Count***
220 COUNT = COUNT + 1
230 RETURN
240 ' *** End of Program ***
```

c. Assume that PRINCIPAL is assigned the value 100 and RATE is assigned the value 15.

```
1000 ' Exercise 1.c
1010 ' ************************
1020 ' *        Main Module      *
1030 ' ************************
1040 GOSUB 2000   ' Accept Operator Input
1050 GOSUB 3000   ' Compute Amount
1060 GOSUB 4000   ' Display Amount
1070 END
1080 '
2000 ' ************************
2010 ' * Accept Operator Input *
2020 ' ************************
2030 CLS : KEY OFF  ' Clear Screen
2040 INPUT "Principal ===> ", PRINCIPAL
2050 INPUT "Rate in % ===> ", RATE
2060 RETURN
2070 '
3000 ' ************************
3010 ' *      Compute Amount     *
3020 ' ************************
3030 RATE = RATE / 100
3040 AMOUNT = PRINCIPAL + RATE * PRINCIPAL
3050 RETURN
3060 '
4000 ' ************************
4010 ' *      Display Amount     *
4020 ' ************************
4030 PRINT USING "Amount ======> #,###.##"; AMOUNT
4040 RETURN
4050 ' ***** End of Program ****
```

2. Is the following partial program invalid? If it is invalid, indicate why.

```
1000 ' Exercise 2
1010 ' **** Main Module *****
     .
     .
     .
1100 GOSUB 2000
1110 '
2000 ' *** Compute Square ***
2010 X = X ^ 2
2020 RETURN
2030 ' *** End of Program ***
```

3. Write a sequence of LOCATE and PRINT statements that will display the word Retail beginning in column 12 of row 15.

4. Write a series of statements that will display the number 22 in column 22 of row 22.

5. Consider the valid program listed below. What is displayed when it is executed?

```
100 ' Exercise 5
110 LESS50 = 0
120 BETWEEN50.100 = 0
130 GREATER100 = 0
140 READ NUM
150 FOR I = 1 TO NUM
160    READ SCORE
170    IF SCORE >= 0 AND SCORE < 50 THEN LESS50 = LESS50 + 1
180    IF SCORE >= 50 AND SCORE <= 100 THEN BETWEEN50.100 = BETWEEN50.100 + 1
190    IF SCORE > 100 THEN GREATER100 = GREATER100 + 1
200 NEXT I
210 PRINT LESS50, BETWEEN50.100, GREATER100
220 DATA 10, 150, 99, 100, 50, 0, 25, 88
230 DATA 42, 101, 10
240 END
```

6. At what column and row is the cursor after the following two statements are executed?

```
600 LOCATE 15, 34
610 LOCATE 17
```

7. Identify the syntax and logic error(s), if any, in each of the following:
   a. 700 FOR X = 1 TO 6 STEP -1
   b. 710 FOR AMT = 1 TO SQ
   c. 720 FOR T$ = 0 TO 7
   d. 730 FOR VALUE = 10 TO 1
   e. 740 FOR H = A TO B STEP -B

8. How many times does the PRINT statement execute when the following program is executed?

```
800 ' Exercise 8
810 FOR J = 1 TO 30
820    FOR N = 1 TO 20
830       FOR I = 1 TO 3
840          PRINT J, N, I
850       NEXT I
860    NEXT N
870 NEXT J
880 END
```

9. Explain the purpose of the following statement. What are the colons used for?

```
900 BEEP : BEEP : BEEP : BEEP
```

STUDENT ASSIGNMENTS

STUDENT ASSIGNMENT 1: Weekly Pay Rate Table

Instructions: Design and code a top-down BASIC program, such as the one on page MB75 in Figure 4-18, to generate the weekly pay rate table shown under OUTPUT. Request that the user enter through the keyboard an hourly rate between $3.35 and $30.00, inclusive. Validate the entry. Use a For loop to generate a table of 10 hourly rates in increments of $0.50 and the corresponding weekly rates. A weekly rate is equal to 40 times the hourly rate. After the table displays, request the user to enter the letter Y to generate another table or the letter N to terminate the program. Use the following top-down chart as a guide to solving this problem:

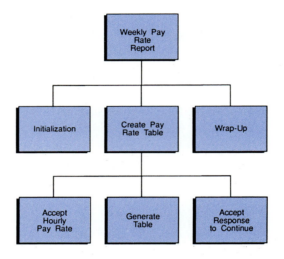

INPUT: Use the following sample data:

Table 1 – Hourly rate $6.75
Table 2 – Hourly rate $22.50

OUTPUT: The following results are displayed for the Table 1 data:

```
Initial Pay Rate (3.35 <= Cost <= 30.00) ·······> 6.75

        Table of Hourly and Weekly Rates

        Hourly                  Weekly
        Rate                    Rate
        ------                  ------
          6.75                  270.00
          7.25                  290.00
          7.75                  310.00
          8.25                  330.00
          8.75                  350.00
          9.25                  370.00
          9.75                  390.00
         10.25                  410.00
         10.75                  430.00
         11.25                  450.00

Enter Y to generate another table, else N ······> Y
```

STUDENT ASSIGNMENT 2: Metric Conversion Table

Instructions: Design and code a top-down BASIC program, such as the one on page MB75 in Figure 4-18, to generate a metric conversion table as shown under OUTPUT on the next page in the printout. Request that the user enter through the keyboard an initial metric value, a limit metric value, and an increment metric value. Validate each entry. The initial metric value must be between 1 and 1,500, inclusive. The limit metric value must be greater than the initial metric value and less than 2,000. The increment metric value must be greater than zero and less than or equal to 100.

Use a For loop to generate a table of the metric values between the initial metric value and limit metric value. For each metric value, print the equivalent yards, feet, and inches. There are 39.37 inches in a meter, 12 inches in a foot, and 3 feet in a yard. After the table prints, request the user to enter the letter Y to generate another table or the letter N to terminate the program. Use the following top-down chart as a guide to solving this problem:

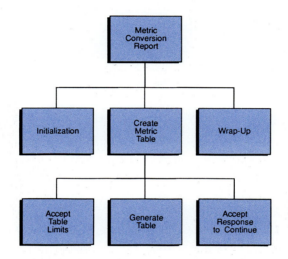

Before you print each table, use the following statement to move the paper in the printer to the top of the next page:

```
LPRINT CHR$(12);
```

This LPRINT statement prints the value of the function CHR$(12), which is the form feed character.

INPUT: Use the following sample data:

Table 1 – Initial meters 100, Limit meters 200, Increment meters 10
Table 2 – Initial meters 140, Limit meters 160, Increment meters 2

OUTPUT: The following results display on the screen for the Table 1 data:

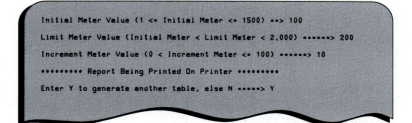

Student Assignment 2 (continued)

The following results are printed on the printer for the Table 1 data:

```
          Metric Conversion Table

Meters       Yards       Feet      Inches
------       -----       ----      ------
100.00      109.36      328.08    3,937.00
110.00      120.30      360.89    4,330.70
120.00      131.23      393.70    4,724.40
130.00      142.17      426.51    5,118.10
140.00      153.11      459.32    5,511.80
150.00      164.04      492.13    5,905.50
160.00      174.98      524.93    6,299.20
170.00      185.91      557.74    6,692.90
180.00      196.85      590.55    7,086.60
190.00      207.79      623.36    7,480.30
200.00      218.72      656.17    7,874.00

End of Table
```

PROJECT 5

MICROSOFT BASIC

Sequential File Processing

OBJECTIVES

You will have mastered the material in this project when you can:

◆ Define the term data file

◆ Describe the two forms of file organization (sequential and random) available in BASIC

◆ State the purpose of the OPEN and CLOSE statements

◆ Discuss techniques for creating sequential files

◆ State the purpose of the WRITE #n statement

◆ State the purpose of the INPUT #n statement

◆ State the purpose of the EOF(n) function

In the first four projects we emphasized the importance of integrating data into the program. You learned that data can be entered into a program through the use of the INPUT statement or the READ and DATA statements. This project presents a third method for entering data—the use of data files. With data files, the data is stored in auxiliary storage rather than in the program itself. This technique is used primarily for dealing with large amounts of data.

BASIC includes a set of file-handling statements that allow a user to do the following:

■ Open a file
■ Read data from a file
■ Write data to a file
■ Test for the end-of-file
■ Close a file

FILE ORGANIZATION

◆ BASIC provides for two types of file organization: sequential and random. A file that is organized sequentially is called a **sequential file** and is limited to sequential processing. This means that the records can be processed only in the order in which they are placed in the file. Conceptually, a sequential file is identical to the use of DATA statements within a BASIC program.

The second type of file organization, **random files**, allows you to process the records in the file in any order. If the fifth record is required and it is stored in a random file, then the program can access it without reading the first four records. Random files are not covered in this project.

CREATING A SEQUENTIAL DATA FILE

◆ This section presents the OPEN, WRITE #n, and CLOSE statements. These statements are used to create a sequential data file. The OPEN statement is used to activate the file. The WRITE #n statement is used to write a record to the file. And the CLOSE statement is used to deactivate the file.

Opening Sequential Files

Before any file can be read from or written to, it must be opened by the OPEN statement. The OPEN statement identifies by name the file to be processed. It indicates whether the file is to be read from or written to. It also assigns the file a filenumber that can be used by statements that need to reference the file in question.

The general form of the OPEN statement is shown in Figure 5-1.

OPEN filespec FOR mode AS #filenumber

where **filespec** is the name of the file;
mode is one of the following:
    APPEND opens the file so that records can be added to the end of the file;
    INPUT opens the file to read beginning with the first record;
    OUTPUT opens the file to write records; and
filenumber is a numeric expression whose value is between 1 and 3.

FIGURE 5-1   The general form of the OPEN statement

As described in Figure 5-1, a sequential data file may be opened for input, output, or append. If a file is opened for input, the program can only read records from it. If a file is opened for output, the program can only write records to it. The Append mode allows you to write records to the end of a file that already has records in it. Figure 5-2 illustrates several OPEN statements.

EXAMPLE	STATEMENT
1	100 OPEN "B:PAYROLL.DAT" FOR OUTPUT AS #3
2	200 OPEN "ACCOUNT.DAT" FOR APPEND AS #2
3	300 OPEN FILENAME$ FOR OUTPUT AS #1
4	400 OPEN "PART.DAT" FOR INPUT AS #1

FIGURE 5-2   Examples of OPEN statements

The OPEN statement in Example 1 in Figure 5-2 opens PAYROLL.DAT on the B drive for output as filenumber 3. Since it is opened for output, you can only write records to PAYROLL.DAT. If you attempt to read a record, the computer will display a diagnostic message.

Example 2 opens the data file ACCOUNT.DAT for append as filenumber 2. Records can only be written to a data file opened for append. If ACCOUNT.DAT exists, records are written in sequence after the last record. If ACCOUNT.DAT does not exist, the computer creates it and the data file is treated as if it were open for output.

Example 3 in Figure 5-2 shows that in an OPEN statement you can use a string variable as the data file name. The assumption is that you will assign a file name to the string variable before the OPEN statement is executed.

Example 4 opens the data file PART.DAT on the default drive for input as filenumber 1. A file opened for input means we plan to read data from it. Later in this project we will show you how data can be read from a data file.

Closing Sequential Files

When a program is finished reading or writing to a file, it must close the file with the CLOSE statement. The CLOSE statement terminates the association between the file and the filenumber assigned in the OPEN statement. If a file is being written to, the CLOSE statement ensures that the last record is written to the data file.

The general form of the CLOSE statement is shown in Figure 5-3.

FIGURE 5-3
The general form of the
CLOSE statement

```
CLOSE

or

CLOSE #filenumber₁, ..., #filenumberₙ
```

The CLOSE statement terminates access to a data file. For example, CLOSE #1 causes the data file assigned to filenumber 1 to be closed. Any other files previously opened by the program remain open. Following the close of a specified file, the filenumber may be assigned again to the same file or to a different file by an OPEN statement. The keyword CLOSE without any filenumber, closes all opened data files.

When executed, the END statement closes all opened files before terminating execution of the program.

Writing Data to a Sequential File

To write data to a sequential file, we use the WRITE #n statement. The WRITE #n statement writes data in a format required by the INPUT #n statement. The format requirement is similar to that of the READ and DATA statements—all data items are separated by commas. The WRITE #n statement goes even one step further by surrounding all string data items written to the file with quotation marks.

The general form of the WRITE #n statement is shown in Figure 5-4.

FIGURE 5-4
The general form of the
WRITE #n statement

```
WRITE #filenumber, variable₁, variable₂, ..., variableₙ
```

Consider the WRITE #n statement in Figure 5-5. Assume that PART.NO$ = 129, DESCRIPTION$ = Hex Bolt, ON.HAND = 200, and WHOLESALE = 1.26. The WRITE #n statement transmits the record shown to the sequential file assigned to filenumber 1. The WRITE #n statement causes a comma to be placed between the data items in the record. Quotation marks are placed around the values of the string variables PART.NO$ and DESCRIPTION$, and a carriage return character ↵ is appended to the last data item written to form the record.

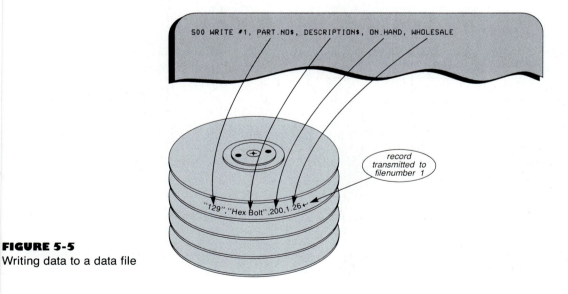

FIGURE 5-5
Writing data to a data file

SAMPLE PROGRAM 5A — CREATING A SEQUENTIAL DATA FILE

◆ In this sample program we create a sequential data file (PART.DAT) on the B drive from the part data shown in Figure 5-6. The data must be written in a format that is consistent with the INPUT #n statement. We use a series of LOCATE, PRINT, and INPUT statements to display the screen on the screen layout form shown in Figure 5-7. As part of the Wrap-Up module, the number of records written to PART.DAT is displayed.

PART NUMBER	DESCRIPTION	ON HAND	WHOLESALE PRICE
323	Canon PC-25	12	$799.92
432	Timex Watch	53	27.95
567	12 Inch Monitor	34	50.30
578	Epson Printer	23	179.95
745	6 Inch Frying Pan	17	9.71
812	Mr. Coffee	39	21.90
923	4-Piece Toaster	7	17.57

FIGURE 5-6 The data to be written to the sequential file PART.DAT

Notice that we are not validating the data entered through the keyboard in this sample program so that we can present a clear-cut example of how to create a sequential file. In a production environment, reasonableness checks are always considered for the part number, description, on hand, and wholesale price. You should always validate data before writing it to a file.

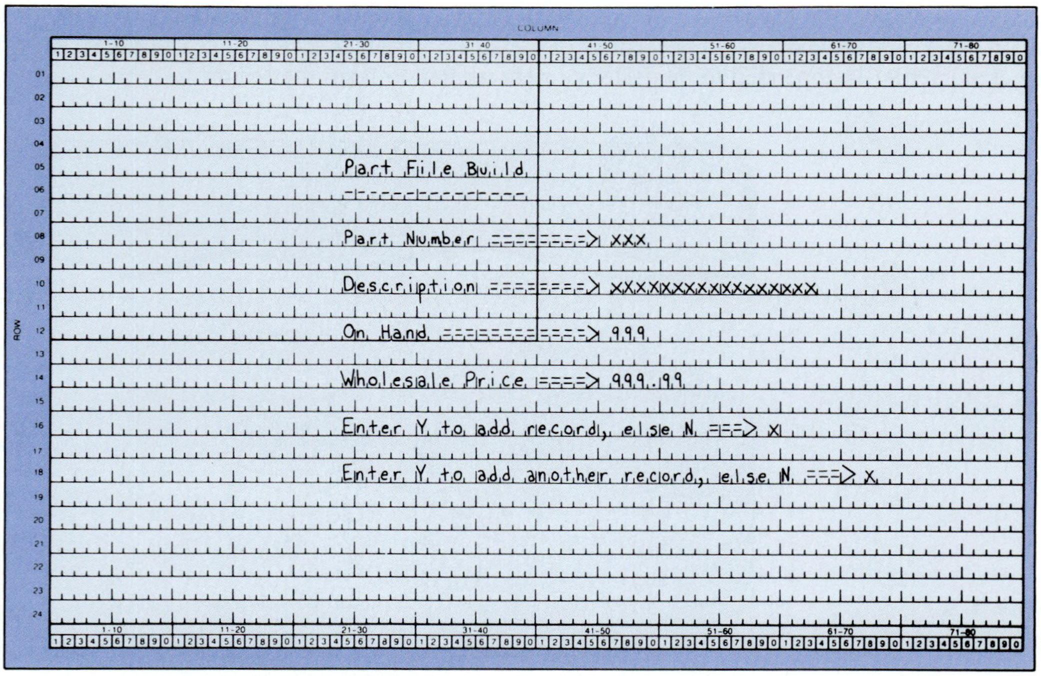

FIGURE 5-7 Screen layout form for Sample Program 5A

A top-down chart, a program flowchart for each module, a program solution, and a discussion of the program solution follow.

Top-Down Chart and Program Flowcharts

Figure 5-8 illustrates the top-down chart and corresponding program flowcharts for each module in Sample Program 5A. In the Initialization module, the record counter is initialized to zero, the data file, PART.DAT is opened, and the twenty-fifth line on the screen is turned off. The Do-Until loop in the Build File module executes until the user indicates that there are no more records to enter. Within the Do-Until loop, a part record is accepted through the keyboard. After each record is entered, the user must enter the letter Y to add the record. This entry gives the user the opportunity to cancel the record while it is displayed on the screen, but before it is added to PART.DAT. After all the records are entered, the Wrap-Up module displays the number of records written to PART.DAT.

In the program flowcharts, notice that the OPEN, WRITE #n, and CLOSE statements are represented by the Input/Output symbol (parallelogram).

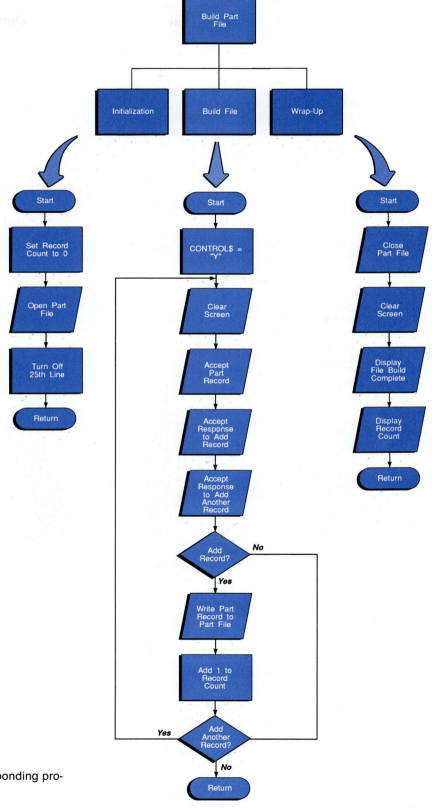

FIGURE 5-8 A top-down chart and corresponding program flowcharts for Sample Program 5A

The BASIC Program

The program in Figure 5-9 corresponds to the top-down chart and program flowcharts in Figure 5-8.

```
1000 ' ************************************************************
1010 ' *   Sample Program 5A                 September 15, 1994  *
1020 ' *   Build Part File                                       *
1030 ' *   J. S. Quasney                                         *
1040 ' *                                                         *
1050 ' *   This program builds the data file PART.DAT.           *
1060 ' *   The user enters each part record through the keyboard. *
1070 ' *   After the record is entered, it is written to PART.DAT. *
1080 ' *       The number of records written to PART.DAT is      *
1090 ' *   displayed as part of the Wrap-Up module.              *
1100 ' *                                                         *
1110 ' *   Variables:  PART.NO$         -- Part number           *
1120 ' *               DESCRIPTION$     -- Part number           *
1130 ' *               ON.HAND          -- Part description      *
1140 ' *               WHOLESALE        -- Number on hand        *
1150 ' *               RECORD.COUNT     -- Wholesale price of part *
1160 ' *                                   PART.DAT              *
1170 ' *               ADD.REC$         -- Indicates if record is to *
1180 ' *                                   be written to PART.DAT *
1190 ' *               CONTROL$         -- Controls Do-Until loop *
1200 ' ************************************************************
1210 '
1220 ' ************************************************************
1230 ' *                    Main Module                          *
1240 ' ************************************************************
1250 GOSUB 2000   ' Call Initialization
1260 GOSUB 3000   ' Call Build File
1270 GOSUB 4000   ' Call Wrap-Up
1280 END
1290 '
2000 ' ************************************************************
2010 ' *                   Initialization                       *
2020 ' ************************************************************
2030 RECORD.COUNT = 0
2040 OPEN "B:PART.DAT" FOR OUTPUT AS #1
2050 KEY OFF   ' Turn off 25th line on screen
2060 RETURN
2070 '
```

FIGURE 5-9 Sample Program 5A

FIGURE 5-9
(continued)

```
3000 ' ************************************************************
3010 ' *                        Build File                        *
3020 ' ************************************************************
3030 LET CONTROL$ = "Y"
3040 WHILE CONTROL$ = "Y" OR CONTROL$ = "y"
3050    CLS  ' Clear Screen
3060    LOCATE 5, 25: PRINT "Part File Build"
3070    LOCATE 6, 25: PRINT "---------------"
3080    LOCATE 8, 25: INPUT "Part Number =======> ", PART.NO$
3090    LOCATE 10, 25: INPUT "Description =======> ", DESCRIPTION$
3100    LOCATE 12, 25: INPUT "On Hand ===========> ", ON.HAND
3110    LOCATE 14, 25: INPUT "Wholesale Price ===> ", WHOLESALE
3120    LOCATE 16, 25: INPUT "Enter Y to add record, else N ===> ", ADD.REC$
3130    IF ADD.REC$ = "Y" OR ADD.REC$ = "y"
            THEN WRITE #1, PART.NO$, DESCRIPTION$, ON.HAND, WHOLESALE :
                 RECORD.COUNT = RECORD.COUNT + 1
3140    LOCATE 18, 25
3150    INPUT "Enter Y to add another record, else N ===> ", CONTROL$
3160 WEND
3170 RETURN
3180 '
4000 ' ************************************************************
4010 ' *                        Wrap-Up                           *
4020 ' ************************************************************
4030 CLOSE #1
4040 CLS  ' Clear Screen
4050 LOCATE 10, 15: PRINT "Creation of PART.DAT is Complete"
4060 LOCATE 14, 15
4070 PRINT "Total Number of Records in PART.DAT ===>"; RECORD.COUNT
4080 RETURN
4090 '
4100 ' ******************** End of Program ********************
```

Discussion of the Program Solution

When Sample Program 5A is executed, line 2040 of the Initialization module opens PART.DAT for output on the B drive as filenumber 1. In the Build File module, lines 3060 through 3150 of the Do-Until loop accept data values through the keyboard. The display due to the execution of these lines for the first record entered by the operator is shown in Figure 5-10. Notice the two messages at the bottom of the screen. The first message (displayed due to line 3120) gives the operator the opportunity to reject the transaction by assigning ADD.REC$ a value other than Y (or y). The second message (displayed due to line 3150) requests that the operator enter a Y (or y) to add another record to the part file.

Owing to line 3130, the part record is added by the WRITE #n statement if ADD.REC$ is equal to Y (or y). Line 3040 controls the Do-Until loop. If CONTROL$ equals Y (or y), then the loop continues. If CONTROL$ is equal to any other value, then control returns to line 1270 in the Main Module.

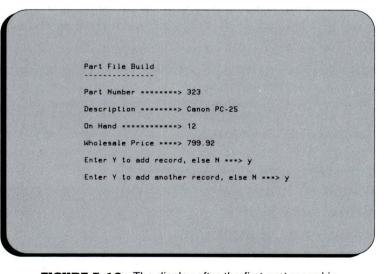

```
Part File Build
---------------

Part Number ========> 323

Description =========> Canon PC-25

On Hand =============> 12

Wholesale Price =====> 799.92

Enter Y to add record, else N ===> y

Enter Y to add another record, else N ===> y
```

FIGURE 5-10 The display after the first part record is entered due to the execution of Sample Program 5A

The WRITE #n statement in line 3130 writes the record to the sequential file PART.DAT in a format that is consistent with the INPUT #n statement. Figure 5-11 shows the format of the data written to PART.DAT by Sample Program 5A.

```
"323","Canon PC-25",12,799.92
"432","Timex Watch",53,27.95
"567","12 Inch Monitor",34,50.3
"578","Epson Printer",23,179.95
"745","6 Inch Frying Pan",17,9.71
"812","Mr. Coffee",39,21.9
"923","4-Piece Toaster",7,17.57
```

FIGURE 5-11   A listing of PART.DAT created by Sample Program 5A

In the Wrap-Up module, line 4030 closes PART.DAT. This ensures that the last record entered by the operator is physically written to the data file on auxiliary storage. Figure 5-12 shows the display due to lines 4040 through 4070 of the Wrap-Up module.

```
Creation of PART.DAT is Complete

Total Number of Records in PART.DAT ---> 7
```

FIGURE 5-12   The display due to the execution of the Wrap-Up module in Sample Program 5A

READING DATA FROM A SEQUENTIAL DATA FILE

The INPUT #n statement is used to read data from a data file that has been created by using the WRITE #n statement. The EOF function is used to determine when all the records have been processed. The following sections describe how the INPUT #n statement and EOF function work.

The INPUT #n Statement

The INPUT #n statement is similar to the READ statement except that it reads data from a data file instead of from DATA statements. In the following partial program,

```
2080 OPEN "PART.DAT" FOR INPUT AS #1
      .
      .
      .
3040 INPUT #1, PART.NO$, DESCRIPTION$, ON.HAND, WHOLESALE
```

the computer reads four data items from the sequential file PART.DAT.

The general form of the INPUT #n statement is shown in Figure 5-13.

```
INPUT #filenumber, variable₁, variable₂, ..., variableₙ
```

FIGURE 5-13   The general form of the INPUT #n statement

The EOF Function

When a sequential data file that was opened for output is closed, the computer automatically adds an end-of-file mark after the last record written to the file. Later, when the same sequential file is opened for input, you can use the EOF(n) function to test for the end-of-file mark. The n indicates the filenumber assigned to the file in the OPEN statement.

If the EOF function senses the end-of-file mark, it returns a value of –1 (true). Otherwise, it returns a value of 0 (false). Hence, the EOF function can be used in a WHILE statement to control the loop. For example, consider the partial program in Figure 5-14. In line 3030, the EOF(1) function is used to control the Do-While loop. Each time the WHILE statement is executed, the computer checks to see whether the data pointer is pointing to the end-of-file mark in PART.DAT.

```
2080 OPEN "B:PART.DAT" FOR INPUT AS #1
       .
       .
       .
3030 WHILE NOT EOF(1)
3040    INPUT #1, PART.NO$, DESCRIPTION$, ON.HAND, WHOLESALE
3050    LET RECORD.COUNT = RECORD.COUNT + 1
3060    LET TOTAL.ON.HAND = TOTAL.ON.HAND + ON.HAND
3070    LET PART.COST = ON.HAND * WHOLESALE
3080    LET TOTAL.PART.COST = TOTAL.PART.COST + PART.COST
3090    LPRINT USING DL1$; PART.NO$, DESCRIPTION$, ON.HAND,
                           WHOLESALE, PART.COST
3100 WEND
```

FIGURE 5-14   Using the EOF function to test for end-of-file

When using the EOF function, it is important to organize your program so that the test for the end-of-file precedes the execution of the INPUT #n statement. In Figure 5-14, notice that only one INPUT #n statement (line 3040) is used, and that this statement is placed inside at the top of the Do-While loop. This is different from our previous programs which used two READ statements—one prior to the Do-While loop and one at the bottom of the Do-While loop.

The logic in Figure 5-14 also works when the file is empty (that is, when the file contains no records). If the PART.DAT file is empty, the OPEN statement (line 2080) in the partial program still opens the file for input. However, when the WHILE statement (line 3030) is executed, the EOF function immediately detects the end-of-file mark on the empty file, thereby causing control to pass to the statement following the corresponding WEND statement in line 3100.

SAMPLE PROGRAM 5B — PROCESSING A SEQUENTIAL DATA FILE

◆ In this sample program we will show you how to read data and generate a report using the part file (PART.DAT) built by Sample Program 5A. The display shown in Figure 5-15 ⓐ instructs the user to prepare the printer to receive the report. The report shown in Figure 5-15 ⓑ contains a detail line for each part number. The total cost for each part is determined by multiplying the number on hand by the wholesale price.

As part of the end-of-job routine, the sample program prints the number of part records processed, total number of parts in inventory, and the total cost of all the parts.

ⓐ **SCREEN DISPLAY**

```
Set the paper in the printer to the top of page

Press the Enter key when the printer is ready...

End of Job
```

ⓑ **PRINTED REPORT**

```
                    Part Cost Report

Part                                Wholesale      Part
No.     Description     On Hand     Price          Cost
----    -----------     -------     ---------      ----
323     Canon PC-25         12       799.92     9,599.04
432     Timex Watch         53        27.95     1,481.35
567     12 Inch Monitor     34        50.30     1,710.20
578     Epson Printer       23       179.95     4,138.85
745     6 Inch Frying P     17         9.71       165.07
812     Mr. Coffee          39        21.90       854.10
923     4-Piece Toaster      7        17.57       122.99
                        -------                 ---------
                            185                 18,071.60

Total Number of Parts =====>    7

End of Job
```

FIGURE 5-15 The screen display ⓐ and printed report ⓑ generated by Sample Program 5B

A top-down chart, a program flowchart for each module, a program solution, and a discussion of the program solution follow.

Top-Down Chart and Program Flowcharts

Figure 5-16 illustrates the top-down chart and corresponding program flowcharts for each module in Sample Program 5B.

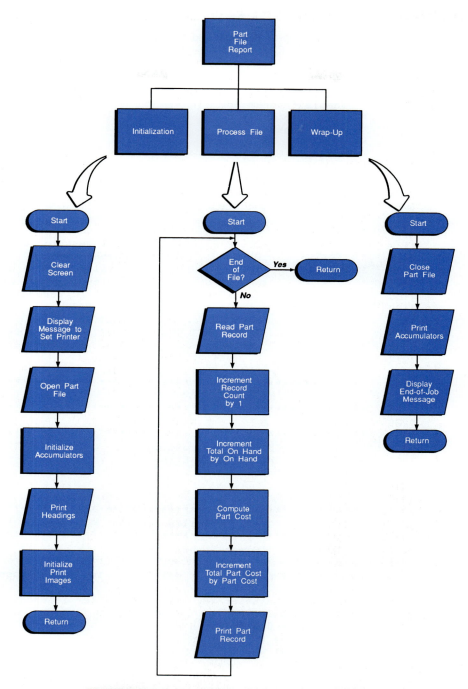

FIGURE 5-16   A top-down chart and corresponding program flowcharts for Sample Program 5B

The BASIC Program

The program in Figure 5-17 corresponds to the top-down chart and program flowcharts in Figure 5-16.

FIGURE 5-17
Sample Program 5B

```
1000 ' ************************************************************
1010 ' *  Sample Program 5B                      September 15, 1994  *
1020 ' *  Part File Report                                          *
1030 ' *  J. S. Quasney                                             *
1040 ' *                                                            *
1050 ' *  This program reads records from the data file PART.DAT    *
1060 ' *  and generates a report on the printer.                    *
1070 ' *       The number of part records processed, total pieces   *
1080 ' *  in inventory, and the total cost are printed as part of   *
1090 ' *  the Wrap-Up module.                                       *
1100 ' *                                                            *
1110 ' *  Variables:   PART.NO$         -- Part number               *
1120 ' *               DESCRIPTION$     -- Part description           *
1130 ' *               ON.HAND          -- Number on hand            *
1140 ' *               TOTAL.ON.HAND    -- Total pieces on hand      *
1150 ' *               WHOLESALE        -- Wholesale price of part   *
1160 ' *               RECORD.COUNT     -- Count of records added to *
1170 ' *                                   PART.DAT                  *
1180 ' *               PART.COST        -- Cost of parts             *
1190 ' *               TOTAL.PART.COST  -- Cost of all parts         *
1200 ' *               CONTROL$         -- Response when printer is  *
1210 ' *                                   ready                     *
1220 ' *               DL1$, TL1$, TL2$, TL3$, TL4$  -- Print Images *
1230 ' ************************************************************
1240 '
1250 ' ************************************************************
1260 ' *                       Main Module                          *
1270 ' ************************************************************
1280 GOSUB 2030    ' Call Initialization
1290 GOSUB 3000    ' Call Process File
1300 GOSUB 4000    ' Call Wrap-Up
1310 END
1320 '
2000 ' ************************************************************
2010 ' *                     Initialization                        *
2020 ' ************************************************************
2030 CLS : KEY OFF   ' Clear Screen
2040 LOCATE 10, 20
2050 PRINT "Set the paper in the printer to the top of page."
2060 LOCATE 12, 20
2070 INPUT "Press the Enter key when the printer is ready...", CONTROL$
2080 OPEN "B:PART.DAT" FOR INPUT AS #1
2090 RECORD.COUNT = 0
2100 TOTAL.ON.HAND = 0
2110 TOTAL.PART.COST = 0
2120 LPRINT "                    Part Cost Report"
2130 LPRINT
2140 LPRINT "Part                                  WHOLESALE     Part"
2150 LPRINT "No.      Description       On Hand     Price         Cost"
2160 LPRINT "----     -----------       -------     ---------     ----"
2170 DL1$ = "\ \        \              \    #,###     #,###.## ##,###.##"
2180 TL1$ = "                          -------                 ---------"
2190 TL2$ = "                          ##,###               ###,###.##"
2200 TL3$ = "Total Number of Parts ====>#,###"
2210 TL4$ = "End of Part Report"
2220 RETURN
2230 '
```

FIGURE 5-17
(continued)

```
3000 ' *********************************************************
3010 ' *                        Process File                   *
3020 ' *********************************************************
3030 WHILE NOT EOF(1)
3040     INPUT #1, PART.NO$, DESCRIPTION$, ON.HAND, WHOLESALE
3050     LET RECORD.COUNT = RECORD.COUNT + 1
3060     LET TOTAL.ON.HAND = TOTAL.ON.HAND + ON.HAND
3070     LET PART.COST = ON.HAND * WHOLESALE
3080     LET TOTAL.PART.COST = TOTAL.PART.COST + PART.COST
3090     LPRINT USING DL1$; PART.NO$, DESCRIPTION$, ON.HAND,
                           WHOLESALE, PART.COST
3100 WEND
3110 RETURN
3120 '
4000 ' *********************************************************
4010 ' *                         Wrap-Up                       *
4020 ' *********************************************************
4030 CLOSE #1
4040 LPRINT TL1$
4050 LPRINT USING TL2$; TOTAL.ON.HAND, TOTAL.PART.COST
4060 LPRINT
4070 LPRINT USING TL3$; RECORD.COUNT
4080 LPRINT
4090 LPRINT TL4$
4100 LOCATE 14, 20
4110 PRINT "End of Job"
4120 RETURN
4130 '
4140 ' ******************** End of Program ********************
```

Discussion of the Program Solution

When Sample Program 5B is executed, the screen display and printed report, shown earlier on page MB92 in Figure 5-15, are generated. Considered the following points in the program solution represented by Sample Program 5B in Figure 5-17:

■ Lines 2040 through 2070 in the Initialization module display on the screen instructions to the user to set the paper in the printer and press the Enter key when ready. Notice how the INPUT statement in line 2070 temporarily halts the program until the user has prepared the printer to receive the report.

■ Line 2080 opens the data file PART.DAT on the B drive for input as filenumber 1. Hence, the program can read records from B:PART.DAT.

■ The WHILE statement in line 3030 controls the Do-While loop using a condition made up of the EOF function. The loop continues to execute while it is not end-of-file.

■ Within the Do-While loop, the INPUT #n statement in line 3040 reads a PART.DAT record by referencing filenumber 1 which was specified in the OPEN statement (line 2080). After lines 3050 through 3080 manipulate the data and accumulate totals, line 3090 prints the detail line. Line 3100 returns control to the WHILE statement in line 3030 which tests for the end-of-file mark.

■ When the end-of-file mark is sensed in line 3030, control passes to the RETURN statement in line 3110. Line 3110 returns control to line 1300 in the Main Module. Line 1300 calls the Wrap-Up module, which prints the accumulators and displays an end-of-job message on the screen. Finally, control returns to the END statement in line 1310 and the program terminates execution.

TRY IT YOURSELF EXERCISES

1. Fill in the blanks in the following sentences.
   a. The _____ statement with a mode of _____ must be executed before an INPUT #n statement is executed.
   b. The _____ statement must be executed before a WRITE #n statement is executed.
   c. The _____ function is used to test for the end-of-file mark with a sequential data file.
   d. When records are to be added to the end of a sequential data file, the _____ mode is used in the OPEN statement.
2. Assume COST = 15, DESC$ = Keyboard, and CODE = 4. Using commas, quotation marks, and ↵ for end of record, indicate the makeup of the record written to auxiliary storage by the following WRITE #n statement:

   ```
   200 WRITE #1, COST, DESC$, CODE
   ```

3. Explain why the EOF function should be used in a condition controlling the loop before the INPUT #n statement is executed.
4. A program is to read records from one of three sequential data files: PART1.DAT, PART2.DAT, and PART3.DAT. The three files are stored on the diskette in the A drive. Write three OPEN statements that would allow the program to read records from any of the three sequential files.
5. Which of the following are invalid file-handling statements? Why?
   a. 500 OPEN SEQ$ FOR OUTPUT AS #1
   b. 510 INPUT #1, COST,
   c. 520 WHILE NOT EOF(#2)
   d. 530 CLOSE #1
   e. 540 WRITE #2, A,
   f. 550 OPEN FOR INPUT "INV.DAT" AS #2
   g. 560 WRITE #1, USING "####.##"; COST

STUDENT ASSIGNMENTS

STUDENT ASSIGNMENT 1: Payroll File Build

Instructions: Design and code a top-down BASIC program to build the payroll file PAYROLL.DAT. Use the sample data shown under INPUT. Generate a screen to receive the data similar to the one under OUTPUT. At the end-of-job, display the number of records written to the data file.

INPUT: Use the following sample data:

EMPLOYEE NUMBER	EMPLOYEE NAME	DEPENDENTS	PAY RATE	HOURS WORKED
23A5	Linda Frat	3	6.75	40
45K8	Joe Smit	1	12.50	38.5
56T1	Lisa Ann	1	16.25	48
65R4	Jeff Max	5	17.75	42
73E6	Susan Dex	2	13.50	40
87Q2	Jeff Web	0	22.45	50
91W2	Marci Jean	3	13.45	40
92R4	Jodi Lin	9	11.50	56
94Y2	Amanda Jo	12	12.75	20
96Y7	Niki Rai	3	16.00	42.5

OUTPUT: The sequential data file PAYROLL.DAT is created in auxiliary storage. The results for the first payroll record are shown below on the left. The results below on the right are displayed prior to termination of the program.

```
Payroll File Build
------------------

Employee Number ========> 23A5

Employee Name ==========> Linda Frat

Number of Dependents ===> 3

Rate of Pay ============> 6.75

Hours Worked ===========> 40

Enter Y to add record, else N ===> y

Enter Y to add another record, else N ===> y
```

```
Creation of PAYROLL.DAT is Complete

Total Number of Records in PAYROLL.DAT ===> 10

Job Complete
```

STUDENT ASSIGNMENT 2: Processing a Payroll File

Instructions: Design and code a top-down BASIC program that generates the messages shown on the screen display under OUTPUT and prints the payroll report under OUTPUT. Apply the following conditions:

1. Gross pay = hours worked × hourly rate.
   Overtime (hours worked > 40) are paid at 1.5 times the hourly rate.
2. Federal withholding tax = 0.2 × (gross pay – dependents × 38.46). Assign federal withholding tax a value of zero if the gross pay less the product of the number of dependents and $38.46 is negative.
3. Net pay = gross pay – federal withholding tax.
4. At the end-of-job, print the number of employees processed, total gross pay, total federal withholding tax, and total net pay.
5. Print the report on the printer.

INPUT: Use the sequential data file PAYROLL.DAT created in Student Assignment 1. If you did not do Student Assignment 1, ask your instructor for a copy of PAYROLL.DAT.

OUTPUT: The following screen with messages and prompts is displayed:

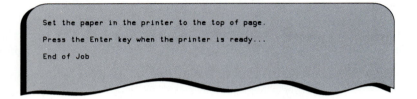

```
Set the paper in the printer to the top of page.

Press the Enter key when the printer is ready...

End of Job
```

The following report prints on the printer:

```
                          Payroll File List

Emp.                          Pay
No.    Name      Dep.  Hours  Rate  Gross Pay  With. Tax  Net Pay
----   ----      ----  -----  ----  ---------  ---------  -------
23A5   Linda Frat  3   40.0   6.75     270.00      30.92   239.08
45K8   Joe Smit    1   38.5  12.50     481.25      88.56   392.69
56T1   Lisa Ann    1   48.0  16.25     845.00     161.31   683.69
65R4   Jeff Max    5   42.0  17.75     763.25     114.19   649.06
73E6   Susan Dex   2   40.0  13.50     540.00      92.62   447.38
87Q2   Jeff Web    0   50.0  22.45   1,234.75     246.95   987.80
91W2   Marci Jean  3   40.0  13.45     538.00      84.52   453.48
92R4   Jodi Lin    9   56.0  11.50     736.00      77.97   658.03
94Y2   Amanda Jo  12   20.0  12.75     255.00       0.00   255.00
96Y7   Niki Rai    3   42.5  16.00     700.00     116.92   583.08

Total Employees ········>       10
Total Gross Pay ········>   6,363.25
Total Tax ··············>   1,013.97
Total Net Pay ··········>   5,349.28

End of Payroll Report
```

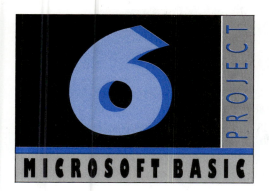

MICROSOFT BASIC

PROJECT

Arrays and Functions

OBJECTIVES

You will have mastered the material in this project when you can:

◆ Discuss the similarities and differences between arrays and simple variables

◆ Describe the use of arrays to perform table processing

◆ Identify the primary uses for arrays in programming

◆ State the purpose of the DIM statement

◆ State the purpose of the OPTION BASE statement

◆ Describe processing of array elements through the use of subscripts

◆ Identify how to declare, load, and manipulate arrays

◆ Identify how to perform table lookups

◆ State the purpose of the INT, SQR, and RND functions

◆ State the purpose of the string functions LEFT\$, LEN, MID\$, and RIGHT\$

◆ State the purpose of the special variables DATE\$ and TIME\$

In the previous projects we used simple variables such as COUNT, EMP.NAME\$, and BALANCE to store and access data in a program. In this project we discuss variables that can store more than one value under the same name. Variables that can hold more than one value at a time are called **arrays**.

An array is often used to store a **table** of organized data. Income tax tables, insurance tables, or sales tax tables are examples of tables that can be stored in an array for processing purposes. Once the table elements are assigned to an array, the array can be searched to extract the proper values.

Functions and special variables are used to handle common mathematical and string operations. For example, it is often necessary in programming to obtain the square root of a number or extract a substring from a string of characters. Without functions, these types of operations would require that you write sophisticated routines in your program. Functions clearly simplify the programming task.

Special variables such as DATE\$ and TIME\$ are automatically set equal to values by BASIC. For example, DATE\$ is equal to the system date. TIME\$ is equal to the system time. You can reference these special variables in LET or PRINT statements.

Although we discuss only the most frequently used functions and special variables, you should be aware that BASIC has over 40 built-in functions and several special variables to aid you in your programming. For a summary of all the functions and special variables available in BASIC, refer to pages R.3 and R.4 of the reference card at the back of this book.

ARRAYS

◆ The banking application in Figure 6-1 illustrates an example of table processing. The account number, name of the account holder, and account balance of individuals who have savings are stored in arrays. When the teller enters account number 20013, the program searches the account number array to find an equal account number.

When the equal account number is found, the corresponding name (Darla Simmons) and the corresponding balance ($932.49) are *pulled* from the table and displayed on the screen.

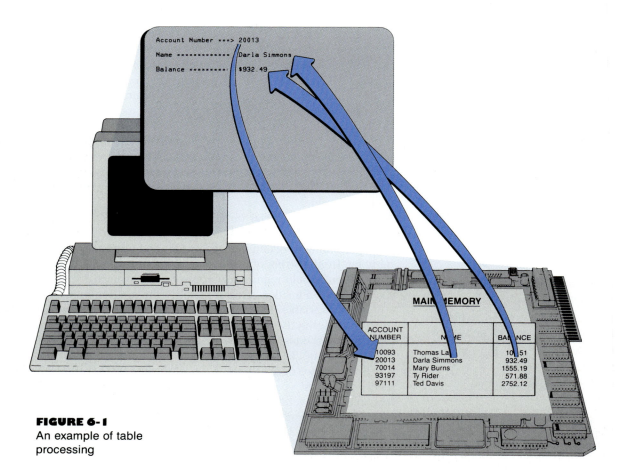

FIGURE 6-1
An example of table
processing

THE DIM STATEMENT

◆ Before arrays can be used, they must be declared in a program. This is the purpose of the DIM statement, also called the dimension statement. The general form of the DIM statement is shown in Figure 6-2.

DIM array name(size), . . . , array name(size)

where **array name** represents a numeric or string variable name, and
size represents the upper-bound value of each array. The size may be an integer or numeric variable for one-dimensional arrays. The size may be a series of integers or a series of numeric variables separated by commas for multidimensional arrays.

FIGURE 6-2 The general form of the DIM statement

Figure 6-3 illustrates several examples of declaring arrays. Example 1 reserves memory for a one-dimensional numeric array TAX, which consists of 6 elements, or memory locations. These elements—TAX(0), TAX(1), TAX(2), TAX(3), TAX(4), and TAX(5)—can be used in a program the same way in which a simple variable can be used. The elements of an array are distinguished from one another by **subscripts** that follow the array name within parentheses.

EXAMPLE	DIM STATEMENT
1	100 DIM TAX(5)
2	200 DIM JOB.CODE$(15), BONUS(15)
3	300 DIM PART.NO$(FIN), DES(FIN)
4	400 DIM FUNCTION.TAX(50, 25)

FIGURE 6-3 Examples of the DIM statement

Example 2 in Figure 6-3 declares two arrays—JOB.CODE$ and BONUS. Both arrays are declared to have 16 elements. Thus, JOB.CODE$(0) through JOB.CODE$(15) and BONUS(0) through BONUS(15) can be referenced in the program containing the DIM statement. JOB.CODE$(16) does not exist according to the DIM statement, and therefore, should not be referenced later in the program. You may declare as many arrays in a DIM statement as required by the program.

Example 3 illustrates that the upper-bound value can be a variable that is assigned a value prior to the execution of the DIM statement. Example 4 illustrates a two-dimensional array. BASIC allows an array to have up to 255 dimensions.

The OPTION BASE Statement

Unless otherwise specified, BASIC allocates the zero element for each one-dimensional array. For two-dimensional arrays, an extra row — the zero row — and an extra column — the zero column — are reserved. Thus,

```
500 DIM MONTH(12), TIME(20, 20)
```

actually reserves 13 elements for the array MONTH and 21 rows and 21 columns for the array TIME. The extra array element is MONTH(0) for array MONTH and the extra row and column is the 0th (read "zeroth") row and the 0th column for the array TIME. Although an additional element, row, or column will not present a problem to your program, the OPTION BASE statement allows you to control the lower-bound values of arrays that are declared. The OPTION BASE statement can be used to set the lower-bound value to 1 instead of the default 0, and this will avoid wasting main memory on unused array elements.

The general form of the OPTION BASE statement is shown in Figure 6-4. The OPTION BASE statement can be used only once in a program and it must precede any DIM statement.

OPTION BASE n

where **n** is either 0 or 1.

FIGURE 6-4 The general form of the OPTION BASE statement

SAMPLE PROGRAM 6 — CUSTOMER ACCOUNT TABLE LOOKUP

◆ In this sample program we implement the banking application shown in Figure 6-1 on page MB100. The account number, name of the account holder, and account balance of customers who have savings accounts are shown in Figure 6-5. The table data is stored in the sequential data file ACCOUNTS.DAT. ACCOUNTS.DAT includes a data item prior to the first account record that is equal to the number of records (5) in the data file.

ACCOUNT NUMBER	CUSTOMER NAME	BALANCE
10093	Thomas Lang	$100.51
20013	Darla Simmons	932.49
70014	Mary Burns	1,555.19
93197	Ty Rider	571.88
97111	Ted Davis	2,752.12

FIGURE 6-5 The table data stored in ACCOUNTS.DAT

The screen display in Figure 6-6 illustrates the output results when the user enters account number 70014. When the user enters the account number, the program should direct the computer to *look up* and display the corresponding customer name and balance. The message at the bottom of the screen in Figure 6-6 asks the user to enter the letter Y to look up another account or the letter N to terminate the program.

If the account number is not found in the table, a diagnostic error displays.

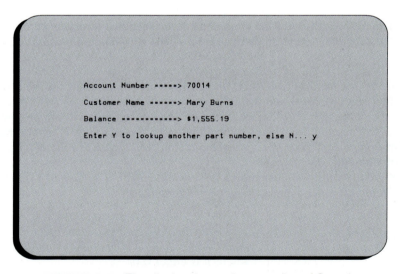

```
Account Number =====> 70014

Customer Name ======> Mary Burns

Balance ============> $1,555.19

Enter Y to lookup another part number, else N... y
```

FIGURE 6-6 The display due to the execution of Sample Program 6 and the entering of account number 70014

A top-down chart, a program flowchart for each module, a program solution, and a discussion of the program solution follow.

Top-Down Chart and Program Flowcharts

The top-down chart and corresponding program flowcharts that illustrate the logic for Sample Program 6 are shown in Figure 6-7.

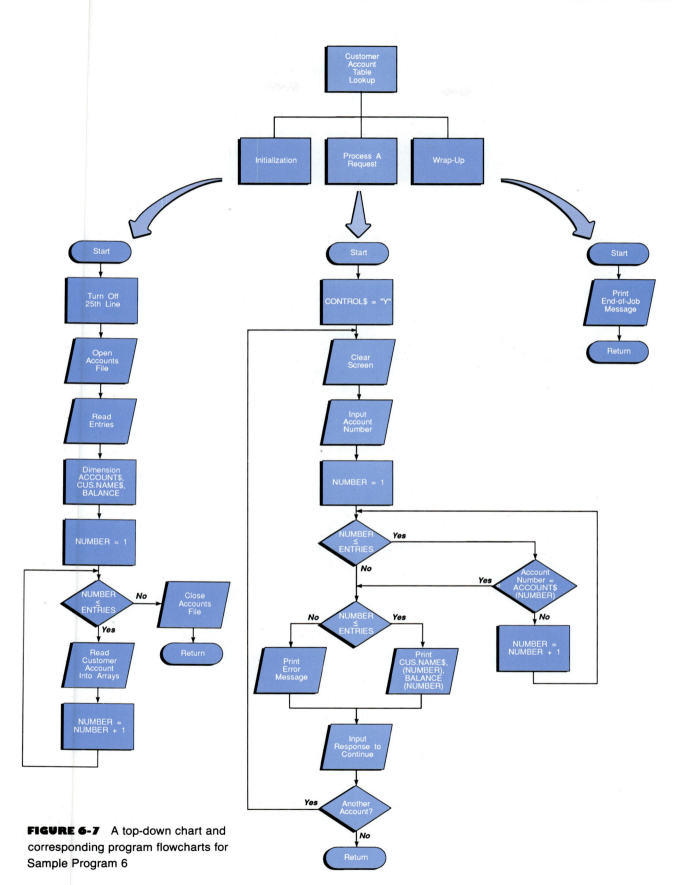

FIGURE 6-7 A top-down chart and corresponding program flowcharts for Sample Program 6

In the Initialization module in Figure 6-7, ACCOUNTS.DAT is opened and the number of records in the account file is read. This value is used to dimension the three arrays that will hold the account information. Next, the same value is used to control a Do-While loop that assigns the account information to the three arrays. After the Do-While loop is finished, ACCOUNTS.DAT is closed.

In the Process A Request module, the program accepts the account number from the user. A Do-While loop is then used to search the array that contains the account numbers. If the search is successful, the customer name and balance display. If the search is unsuccessful, a diagnostic message displays. Finally, the user is asked if he or she wants to enter another account number.

When the user enters something other than the letter Y (or y), control returns to the Main Module. Control then transfers to the Wrap-Up module. The Wrap-Up module displays an end-of-job message.

The BASIC Program

The BASIC code in Figure 6-8 corresponds to the top box in the top-down chart in Figure 6-7. The GOSUB statements call the subordinate modules. Following the return of control from the Wrap-Up module, the END statement terminates execution of the program.

```
1220 ' ***************************************************************
1230 ' *                       Main Module                          *
1240 ' ***************************************************************
1250 GOSUB 2000    ' Call Initialization
1260 GOSUB 3000    ' Call Process A Request
1270 GOSUB 3240    ' Call Wrap-Up
1280 END
1290 '
```

FIGURE 6-8   The Main Module for Sample Program 6

Initialization Module   The Initialization module for Sample Program 6 is shown in Figure 6-9. The primary objective of this module is to load the data in ACCOUNTS.DAT into the arrays. Line 2040 opens ACCOUNTS.DAT on the B drive. Line 2050 assigns the first data item in ACCOUNTS.DAT to the variable ENTRIES. ENTRIES is then assigned the value 5. Line 2060 sets the lower-bound value for all arrays to 1. Line 2070 dimensions the three arrays with an upper-bound value equal to ENTRIES. The For loop in lines 2080 through 2100 reads the data in ACCOUNTS.DAT into the three arrays. Arrays ACCOUNT$, CUS.NAME$, and BALANCE, therefore, contain the data in ACCOUNTS.DAT. Since each array contains data that corresponds to the other arrays, we call them **parallel arrays**. Line 2110 closes ACCOUNTS.DAT before control returns to the Main Module.

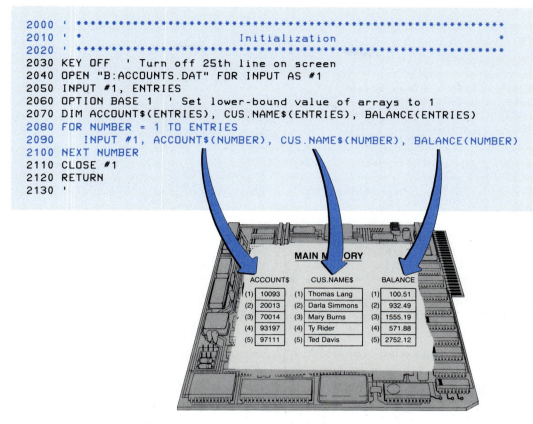

```
2000 ' ****************************************************************
2010 ' *                     Initialization                         *
2020 ' ****************************************************************
2030 KEY OFF  ' Turn off 25th line on screen
2040 OPEN "B:ACCOUNTS.DAT" FOR INPUT AS #1
2050 INPUT #1, ENTRIES
2060 OPTION BASE 1  ' Set lower-bound value of arrays to 1
2070 DIM ACCOUNT$(ENTRIES), CUS.NAME$(ENTRIES), BALANCE(ENTRIES)
2080 FOR NUMBER = 1 TO ENTRIES
2090   INPUT #1, ACCOUNT$(NUMBER), CUS.NAME$(NUMBER), BALANCE(NUMBER)
2100 NEXT NUMBER
2110 CLOSE #1
2120 RETURN
2130 '
```

MAIN MEMORY

	ACCOUNT$		CUS.NAME$		BALANCE
(1)	10093	(1)	Thomas Lang	(1)	100.51
(2)	20013	(2)	Darla Simmons	(2)	932.49
(3)	70014	(3)	Mary Burns	(3)	1555.19
(4)	93197	(4)	Ty Rider	(4)	571.88
(5)	97111	(5)	Ted Davis	(5)	2752.12

FIGURE 6-9   The Initialization module for Sample Program 6

Process A Request Module   After the data in ACCOUNTS.DAT is loaded into the arrays and control passes back to the Main Module, line 1260 transfers control to the Process A Request module (on the next page in Figure 6-10). This module begins by clearing the screen and accepting the account number from the user. The account number is assigned to the variable SEARCH.ARGUMENT$ (line 3070).

```
3000 ' *********************************************************************
3010 ' *                        Process A Request                        *
3020 ' *********************************************************************
3030 CONTROL$ = "Y"
3040 WHILE CONTROL$ = "Y" OR CONTROL$ = "y"
3050    CLS  ' Clear Screen
3060    LOCATE 5, 15
3070    INPUT "Account Number =====> ", SEARCH.ARGUMENT$
3080    FOR NUMBER = 1 TO ENTRIES
3090       IF SEARCH.ARGUMENT$ = ACCOUNT$(NUMBER) THEN 3110
3100    NEXT NUMBER
3110    IF NUMBER <= ENTRIES THEN 3150
3120       LOCATE 7, 15
3130       PRINT "Account Number "; SEARCH.ARGUMENT$; " NOT FOUND"
3140    GOTO 3190
3150       LOCATE 7, 15
3160       PRINT "Customer Name ======> "; CUS.NAME$(NUMBER)
3170       LOCATE 9, 15
3180       PRINT USING "BALANCE ============> $$,###.##"; BALANCE(NUMBER)
3190    LOCATE 11, 15
3200    INPUT "Enter Y to lookup another part number, else N... ", CONTROL$
3210 WEND
3220 RETURN
3230 '
```

FIGURE 6-10 The Process A Request module for Sample Program 6

The For loop in lines 3080 through 3100 of Figure 6-10 searches the ACCOUNT$ array for a match with SEARCH.ARGUMENT$. The IF statement in the For loop (line 3090) compares SEARCH.ARGUMENT$ to the next element in ACCOUNT$ each time through the loop, until a *hit* is made. When a *hit* occurs, the THEN clause of line 3090 causes a premature exit from the For loop and control passes to line 3110. If no *hit* occurs, a normal exit from the For loop also passes control to line 3110.

Line 3110 determines if the search for the account number in ACCOUNT$ was successful. If the search was successful, then NUMBER is less than or equal to ENTRIES. In this case, the customer number and balance from the two corresponding arrays are displayed using the value of NUMBER for the subscript. Figure 6-11 shows the display due to a successful search.

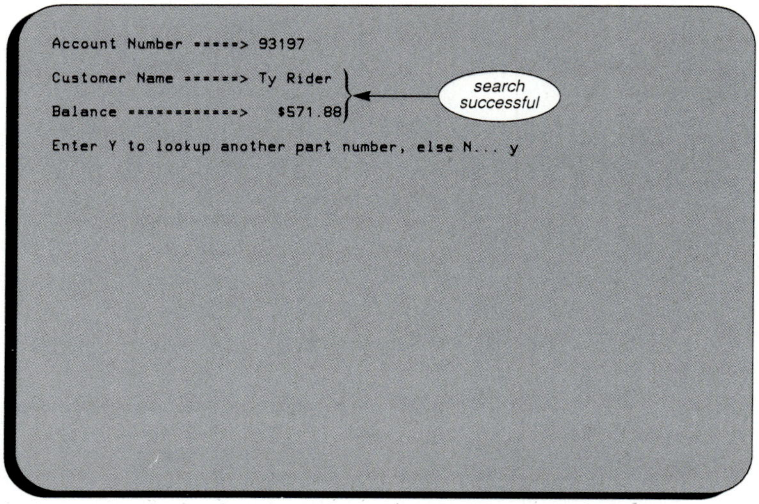

FIGURE 6-11 The display from Sample Program 6 due to entering the account number 93197

If the search is unsuccessful, then NUMBER is greater than ENTRIES and the diagnostic message in line 3130 displays as shown in Figure 6-12. If there is a premature exit from the For loop, the search is successful. If the For loop ends normally, the search is unsuccessful.

```
Account Number ======> 12123

Account Number 12123 NOT FOUND◄————   search
                                      unsuccessful
Enter Y to lookup another part number, else N... y
```

FIGURE 6-12 The display from Sample Program 6 due to entering the invalid account number 12123

After the true or false task in the IF statement (lines 3120 through 3180) is executed, line 3200 requests that the user enter the letter Y to process another account number or the letter N to terminate execution of the program.

The complete BASIC program is shown in Figure 6-13.

```
1000 ' ***************************************************************
1010 ' *    Sample Program 6                    September 15, 1994  *
1020 ' *    Customer Account Table Lookup                          *
1030 ' *    J. S. Quasney                                          *
1040 ' *                                                           *
1050 ' *    This program loads the data in ACCOUNTS.DAT into arrays. *
1060 ' *    The user enters the account number and the program looks *
1070 ' *    up and displays the customer number and account balance. *
1080 ' *         If the account number is not found, then a          *
1090 ' *    diagnostic message is displayed.  After processing a     *
1100 ' *    request, the user is asked if he or she wishes to        *
1110 ' *    display information on another account or terminate the  *
1120 ' *    program.                                                 *
1130 ' *                                                             *
1140 ' *    Variables: ACCOUNT$          -- Account number array     *
1150 ' *               CUS.NAME$         -- Customer name array      *
1160 ' *               BALANCE           -- Customer balance array   *
1170 ' *               SEARCH.ARGUMENT$  -- Account number requested *
1180 ' *               CONTROL$          -- Response to continue     *
1190 ' *               ENTRIES           -- Number of customers      *
1200 ' ***************************************************************
1210 '
1220 ' ***************************************************************
1230 ' *                      Main Module                           *
1240 ' ***************************************************************
1250 GOSUB 2000    ' Call Initialization
1260 GOSUB 3000    ' Call Process A Request
1270 GOSUB 3240    ' Call Wrap-Up
1280 END
1290 '
```

FIGURE 6-13 Sample Program 6 *(continued)*

FIGURE 6-13
(continued)

```
2000 ' *************************************************************
2010 ' *                      Initialization                      *
2020 ' *************************************************************
2030 KEY OFF   ' Turn off 25th line on screen
2040 OPEN "B:ACCOUNTS.DAT" FOR INPUT AS #1
2050 INPUT #1, ENTRIES
2060 OPTION BASE 1  ' Set lower-bound value of arrays to 1
2070 DIM ACCOUNT$(ENTRIES), CUS.NAME$(ENTRIES), BALANCE(ENTRIES)
2080 FOR NUMBER = 1 TO ENTRIES
2090    INPUT #1, ACCOUNT$(NUMBER), CUS.NAME$(NUMBER), BALANCE(NUMBER)
2100 NEXT NUMBER
2110 CLOSE #1
2120 RETURN
2130 '
3000 ' *************************************************************
3010 ' *                    Process A Request                     *
3020 ' *************************************************************
3030 CONTROL$ = "Y"
3040 WHILE CONTROL$ = "Y" OR CONTROL$ = "y"
3050    CLS  ' Clear Screen
3060    LOCATE 5, 15
3070    INPUT "Account Number =====> ", SEARCH.ARGUMENT$
3080    FOR NUMBER = 1 TO ENTRIES
3090       IF SEARCH.ARGUMENT$ = ACCOUNT$(NUMBER) THEN 3110
3100    NEXT NUMBER
3110    IF NUMBER <= ENTRIES THEN 3150
3120       LOCATE 7, 15
3130       PRINT "Account Number "; SEARCH.ARGUMENT$; " NOT FOUND"
3140    GOTO 3190
3150       LOCATE 7, 15
3160       PRINT "Customer Name ======> "; CUS.NAME$(NUMBER)
3170       LOCATE 9, 15
3180       PRINT USING "BALANCE ============> $$,###.##"; BALANCE(NUMBER)
3190    LOCATE 11, 15
3200    INPUT "Enter Y to lookup another part number, else N... ", CONTROL$
3210 WEND
3220 RETURN
3230 '
3240 ' *************************************************************
3250 ' *                        Wrap-Up                           *
3260 ' *************************************************************
3270 LOCATE 13, 15
3280 PRINT "Job Complete"
3290 RETURN
3300 ' ********************* End of Program *********************
```

FUNCTIONS AND SPECIAL VARIABLES

◆ BASIC includes over 40 numeric and string functions and several special variables. Numeric functions are used to handle common mathematical calculations. String functions are used to manipulate strings of characters. Special variables are automatically set equal to values by BASIC. A discussion follows of some of the most often used functions and special variables.

Numeric Functions

Three of the most frequently used numeric functions are the INT, SQR, and RND functions. The purpose of these functions is summarized in Figure 6-14.

FUNCTION	FUNCTION VALUE
INT(X)	Returns the largest integer that is less than or equal to the argument X.
SQR(X)	Returns the square root of the argument X.
RND	Returns a random number greater than or equal to zero and less than 1.

FIGURE 6-14 Frequently used numeric functions

INT Function   The INT function returns a whole number that is less than or equal to the argument. Figure 6-15 shows several examples of the INT function.

VALUE OF VARIABLE	BASIC STATEMENT	RESULT
X = 12.45	100 LET Y = INT(X)	Y = 12
H = 27.89	200 LET G = INT(H + 10)	G = 37
J = -15.67	300 LET K = INT(J)	K = -16

FIGURE 6-15 Examples of the INT function

SQR Function   The SQR function computes the square root of the argument. Figure 6-16 illustrates several examples of the SQR function. The argument for the SQR function must be a non-negative value.

VALUE OF VARIABLE	BASIC STATEMENT	RESULT
Y = 4	400 LET X = SQR(Y)	X = 2
D = 27	500 LET P = SQR(D * 3)	P = 9
E = -16	600 LET U = SQR(E)	Illegal Function Call

FIGURE 6-16 Examples of the SQR function

RND Function   The RND function returns an unpredictable number that is greater than or equal to zero and less than 1. The partial program in Figure 6-17 uses a For loop and the RND function to generate three random numbers, .7132002, .6291881, and .3409873.

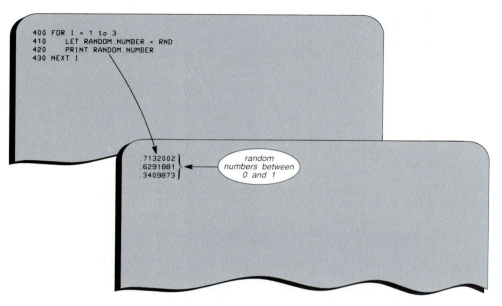

```
400 FOR I = 1 to 3
410    LET RANDOM.NUMBER = RND
420    PRINT RANDOM.NUMBER
430 NEXT I
```

```
.7132002
.6291881
.3409873
```

random numbers between 0 and 1

FIGURE 6-17   An example of the RND function

The INT and RND functions can be used to generate random digits over any range. The following expression generates random numbers between L and U:

```
INT((U - L + 1) * RND + L)
```

For example, to simulate the roll of a six-sided die, we can write the following:

```
610 LET DIE1 = INT((6 - 1 + 1) * RND + 1)
```

   or

```
610 LET DIE1 = INT(6 * RND + 1)
```

In Figure 6-18, the For loop generates five rolls of two dice. The first LET statement represents the roll of one die and the second LET statement represents the roll of the second die.

Each time you run the program in Figure 6-18, it generates the same sequence of random numbers. To generate a new sequence of random numbers each time you execute the program, insert the RANDOMIZE statement at the top of the program. When executed, the RANDOMIZE statement requests that you enter a number between –32768 and 32767. The value you enter is used by the computer to develop a new set of random numbers.

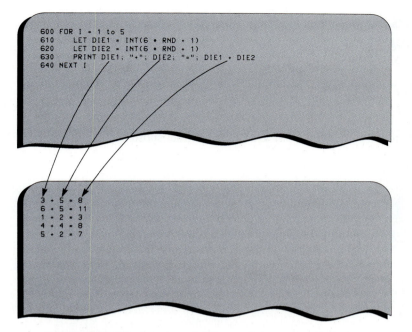

```
600 FOR I = 1 to 5
610    LET DIE1 = INT(6 * RND + 1)
620    LET DIE2 = INT(6 * RND + 1)
630    PRINT DIE1; "+"; DIE2; "="; DIE1 + DIE2
640 NEXT I
```

```
3 + 5 = 8
6 + 5 = 11
1 + 2 = 3
4 + 4 = 8
5 + 2 = 7
```

FIGURE 6-18 An example of a partial program that simulates five rolls of two dice

String Functions

The capability to process strings is important in business applications. In BASIC, you can join two strings together through the use of the concatenation operator (+). For example, the following LET statement:

```
700 LET JOIN$ = "ABC" + "DEF"
```

assigns the variable JOIN$ the value ABCDEF. Besides the concatenation operator, BASIC includes over 20 functions that allow you to manipulate string values.

The most frequently used string functions are shown in Figure 6-19.

FUNCTION	FUNCTION VALUE
LEFT$(S$, X)	Returns the leftmost X characters of the string argument S$.
LEN(S$)	Returns the number of characters in the string argument S$.
MID$(S$, P, X)	Returns X characters from the string argument S$ beginning at position P.
RIGHT$(S$, X)	Returns the rightmost X characters of the string argument S$.

FIGURE 6-19 Frequently used string functions

Use of the LEFT$, LEN, MID$, and RIGHT$ Functions

The LEN(S$) function returns the number of characters in S$. For example, the following LET statement assigns LENGTH the value 5 because there are five characters in the string BASIC:

```
800 LET LENGTH = LEN("BASIC")
```

The LET statement LET NUMBER = LEN(DATE$) assigns NUMBER the value 10 because there are 10 characters in the system date (mm/dd/yyyy).

The LEFT$, MID$, and RIGHT$ functions are used to extract substrings from a string. Figure 6-20 illustrates several examples of these functions.

VALUE OF VARIABLE	BASIC STATEMENT	RESULT
Assume S$ is equal to GOTO is a four-letter word		
1	100 LET Q$ = LEFT$(S$, 7)	Q$ = GOTO is
2	200 LET W$ = LEFT$(S$, 4)	W$ = GOTO
3	300 LET D$ = RIGHT$(S$, 11)	D$ = letter word
4	400 LET K$ = RIGHT$(S$, 1)	K$ = d
5	500 LET M$ = MID$(S$, 6, 2)	M$ = is
6	600 LET T$ = MID$(S$, 16, 6)	T$ = letter

FIGURE 6-20   Examples of the LEFT$, RIGHT$, and MID$ functions

Special Variables

The special variables DATE$ and TIME$ are equal to the DOS system date and time. For example, if the system date is initialized to September 15, 1994, then the statement PRINT "The date is "; DATE$ displays the following result:

```
The date is 09-15-1994
```

If the system time is equal to 11:44:42, then the statement PRINT "The time is "; TIME$ displays the following result:

```
The time is 11:44:42
```

The system time is maintained in 24-hour notation. That is, 1:30 P.M. displays as 13:30:00.

BASIC also allows the argument to include a function. For example, if the system date is 9/15/94, then the LET statement LET DAY$ = MID$(DATE$, 4, 2) assigns DAY$ the string value 15. If the system time is equal to 10:32:52, then the LET statement LET SECOND$ = MID$(TIME$, 7, 2) assigns SECOND$ the string value 52.

Consider the partial program in Figure 6-21 and the corresponding output results. Lines 100 and 110 display the system date and time. Lines 130 through 150 display on separate lines the substrings month, day, and year. Lines 170 through 190 display on separate lines the substrings hour, minute, and second.

For a complete list of the special variables available in BASIC, see the last page of the reference card at the back of this book.

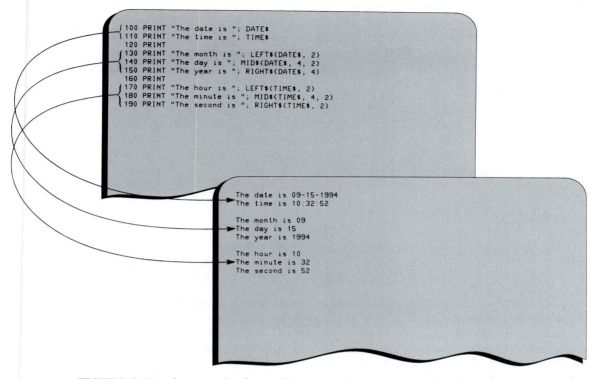

FIGURE 6-21   An example of a partial program that uses string functions. Assume system date is 9/15/94 and system time is 10:32:52

TRY IT YOURSELF EXERCISES

1. What is displayed when the following programs are executed?

   a.
   ```
   100 ' Exercise 1.a
   110 CITY$ = "Los Angeles"
   120 PRINT LEFT$(CITY$, 1) + MID$(CITY$, 5, 1) + " LAW"
   130 END
   ```

   b.
   ```
   100 ' Exercise 1.b
   110 PRINT "Number", "Square", "Square Root"
   120 FOR I = 1 TO 10
   130     PRINT I, I ^ 2, SQR(I)
   140 NEXT I
   150 END
   ```

Try It Yourself Exercises (continued)

2. Assume arrays PART and COST are dimensioned by the statement DIM PART(5), COST(5). Assume that the two arrays were loaded with the following values:

ELEMENT	PART ARRAY	COST ARRAY
1	15	1.23
2	71	2.34
3	92	.25
4	94	1.37
5	99	5.25

Indicate how you would reference the following values using subscripts. For example, .25 can be referenced by COST(3).
a. 71   b. 5.25   c. 2.34   d. 15   e. 1.37   f. 1.23   g. 99

3. Write an OPTION BASE statement and a DIM statement to minimally dimension array X so that subscripts in the range 1 to 900 are valid and array Y so that subscripts in the range 1 to 22 are valid.

4. Given that array G has been declared to have 10 elements (1 to 10), assume that each element of G has a value. Write a partial program that includes a DIM statement to shift all the values up one location. That is, assign G(1) to G(2), G(2) to G(3), and G(10) to G(1).

5. Identify the errors, if any, in each of the following:
   a. 500 DIM AMT(1 TO -1)
   b. 510 DIM BAL (-10)
   c. 520 DIM SALES
   d. 530 DIM (35)X

6. Indicate what each of the following are equal to. Assume PHRASE$ is equal to Aim the arrow carefully.
   a. LEN(PHRASE$)
   b. MID$(PHRASE$, 4, 3)
   c. LEFT$(PHRASE$, 13)
   d. RIGHT$(PHRASE$, 5)

7. Assume that the system date is equal to December 25, 1994 and the system time is equal to 11:12:15. Evaluate the following:
   a. 700 LET X$ = TIME$
   b. 710 LET X$ = MID$(TIME$, 4, 1)
   c. 720 LET X$ = RIGHT$(DATE$, 2)
   d. 730 LET X$ = LEFT$(DATE$, 2)

8. Write a LET statement that assigns NUMBER a random value between 1 and 52.
9. Explain the purpose of the RANDOMIZE statement.
10. What does each of the following equal?
   a. INT(23.46)
   b. SQR(121)
   c. LEN("ABC")
   d. INT(-12.43)
   e. SQR(SQR(81))
   f. SQR(INT(36.57))

STUDENT ASSIGNMENTS

STUDENT ASSIGNMENT 1: Phone Number Lookup

Instructions: Design and code a top-down BASIC program that requests a person's last name and displays the person's telephone number.

Read the data shown in the phone number table under INPUT into parallel arrays from a sequential data file or DATA statements. If you plan to use a sequential data file, ask your instructor for a copy of PHONE.DAT.

Accept a person's last name in lowercase from the user. Search the last name array. If the search is successful, display the corresponding telephone number. If the search is unsuccessful, display a diagnostic message. After the search, ask the user if he or she wants to look up another telephone number. The output results should be similar to the displayed results shown under OUTPUT.

INPUT: Use the following phone number table data. Include a value at the beginning of the file which indicates the number of elements required in the parallel arrays that will hold the names and phone numbers.

Look up the phone numbers of the following individuals: fuqua, bingle, smith, and course.

NAME	PHONE NUMBER
miller	(213) 430–2865
flaming	(213) 866–9082
fuqua	(714) 925–3391
bingle	(805) 402–3376
course	(213) 423–7765

OUTPUT: The following results are displayed for bingle and smith:

```
Person's Name =====> bingle
Phone Number ======> (805) 402-3376
Enter Y to lookup another phone number, Else N... y
```

```
Person's Name =====> smith
The Name smith NOT FOUND
Enter Y to lookup another phone number, Else N... y
```

STUDENT ASSIGNMENT 2: Weight Table Lookup

Instructions: Design and code a top-down BASIC program that accepts a male or female height and displays the average weight ranges for a small-framed, medium-framed, and large-framed person. If the search is unsuccessful, display an error message. The table entries are shown in the height and weight table data under INPUT. The output results are shown under OUTPUT.

INPUT: Use the following height and weight table data. Read the table data into two separate sets of parallel arrays, one for the male weights and one for the female weights, by means of a data file or DATA statements. If you plan to use a sequential data file, ask your instructor for a copy of WEIGHT.DAT. Initialize a variable to nine (the number of different heights for males and for females prior to the DIM statement). Use this variable to dimension the arrays and control any loops that search for heights. Look up the following:

Sex – Male, Height – 72
Sex – Female, Height – 64
Sex – Male, Height – 76
Sex – Female, Height – 72
Sex – Male, Height – 70

MEN

HEIGHT	SMALL FRAME	MEDIUM FRAME	LARGE FRAME
66	124–133	130–143	138–156
67	128–136	134–147	142–161
68	132–141	138–152	147–168
69	136–145	142–156	151–170
70	140–150	146–160	155–174
71	144–154	150–165	159–179
72	148–158	154–170	164–184
73	152–162	158–175	168–189
74	156–167	162–180	173–194

WOMEN

HEIGHT	SMALL FRAME	MEDIUM FRAME	LARGE FRAME
62	102–110	107–119	115–131
63	105–113	110–122	118–134
64	108–116	113–126	121–138
65	111–119	116–130	125–142
66	114–123	120–135	129–148
67	118–127	124–139	133–150
68	122–131	128–143	137–154
69	126–135	132–147	141–158
70	130–140	136–151	145–163

OUTPUT: The following screen displays for the first set of data under INPUT:

```
Person's Sex (M or F) --------> M

Person's Height in Inches
Male 66-74, Female 62-70) ----> 72

Small Frame Weight Range -----> 148-158

Medium Frame Weight Range ----> 154-170

Large Frame Weight Range -----> 164-184

Enter a Y to lookup another weight range, else N... Y
```

Debugging Techniques

Although the top-down approach and structured programming techniques help you to minimize errors, they by no means guarantee error-free programs. Owing to carelessness or insufficient thought, program portions can be constructed which do not work as anticipated and which give erroneous results. When such problems occur, you need techniques to isolate the errors and correct the erroneous program statements.

BASIC can detect many different grammatical errors and can display appropriate diagnostic messages. However, no programming system can detect all errors, since literally hundreds of possible coding errors can be made. Some of these errors can go undetected by BASIC until either an abnormal end occurs during execution or the program terminates with the results in error.

There are several techniques you can use for attempting to discover the portion of the program that is in error. These methods are called **debugging techniques**. The errors themselves are **bugs**, and the activity involved in their detection is **debugging**.

TRACING (TRON AND TROFF)

◆ The TRON (TRace ON) instruction in BASIC provides a means of tracing the path of execution through a program in order to determine which statements are executed. The instruction TROFF (TRace OFF) turns off the tracing. These instructions may be inserted into a program as BASIC statements, or they may be used as system commands before the RUN command is issued. Pressing the F7 key enters the instruction TRON, and pressing the F8 key enters the instruction TROFF.

The TRON instruction activates tracing, and the computer displays the line number of each statement executed. The line numbers appear enclosed in square brackets to prevent them from being confused with other results the program may produce.

For example, if a computer with tracing activated executes a program portion consisting of lines 250, 260, 270, and 280, the output displayed will be as follows:

```
[250] [260] [270] [280]
```

The TROFF instruction deactivates tracing. Both the TRON and TROFF instructions may be used any number of times in a BASIC program.

The program in Figure A-1 has the TRON and TROFF statements in lines 125 and 195. When the RUN command is issued, all statements between lines 125 and 195 are traced, and their line numbers and corresponding output are displayed accordingly.

```
100 ' Program A.1
110 ' Illustrating Use of the
115 ' TRON and TROFF Instructions
120 ' **************************
125 TRON
130 SUM = 0
140 I = 1
150 WHILE I < 4
160     SUM = SUM + I
170     I = I + 1
180     PRINT I; SUM
190 WEND
195 TROFF
200 END

RUN

[130] [140] [150] [160] [170] [180] 2   1
[190] [160] [170] [180]   3   3
[190] [160] [170] [180]   4   6
[190] [195]
```

FIGURE A-1   Using the TRON and TROFF statements

The program in Figure A-2 is similar to the program in Figure A-1. When this program is executed, the computer displays the value of 1 for I again and again. The program has a bug, which results in an infinite loop when the program is run.

```
100 ' Program A.2
110 ' This Program Contains a Bug
120 ' **************************
130 SUM = 0
140 I = 1
150 WHILE I < 4
160     SUM = SUM + I
170     T = I + 1          ' This line contains an error
180     PRINT I; SUM
190 WEND
200 END
```

FIGURE A-2   A program with a bug

If the TRON instruction is used with the program in Figure A-2 as a system command, the following output occurs during tracing:

```
TRON
RUN

[100] [110] [120] [130] [140] [150] [160] [170] [180] 1  1
[190] [160] [170] [180]   1  2
[190] [160] [170] [180]   1  3
[190] [160] [170] [180]   1  4
[190]...
```

From the output, we can see the repetition of the following sequence of line numbers:

```
[190][160][170][180]
```

This output reveals that the program executes lines 160, 170, 180, and 190 repeatedly in the Do-While loop. The condition in the WHILE statement in line 150 cannot be satisfied, since the value of I will always be less than 4. Line 170 has been incorrectly written. In order to satisfy the condition in the WHILE statement, use:

```
170    I = I + 1    instead of:    170    T = I + 1
```

EXAMINING VALUES (STOP, PRINT, AND CONT)

◆ Another useful debugging technique is to stop a program, examine the values of various variables within the program, and then continue the execution of the program. All this can be accomplished through the use of the STOP, PRINT, and CONT (continue) statements. Consider the partial program in Figure A-3.

```
100 ' Program A.3
110 ' Illustrating the Use of STOP, PRINT, and CONT
120 ' **********************************************
130 .
    .
    .
300 V1 = 10 * 12.15
310 A1 = 2 * 24.3
320 S1 = 36.9 / 3
325 STOP
    .
    .
    .
RUN

Break in 325             (displayed when STOP statement is executed)

PRINT V1                 (entered by user)
 121.5                   (displayed result from PRINT statement)

PRINT A1; S1             (entered by user)
 48.6  12.3              (displayed result from PRINT statement)

CONT                     (entered by user)
```

FIGURE A-3 Examining values using the STOP, PRINT, and CONT statements

When the STOP statement executes in line 325, the program stops and the message Break in 325 displays. Now the values of various variables can be examined by using a PRINT statement without a line number.

After the values of V1, A1, and S1 display, the CONT is issued and the remaining program executes. CONT should not be placed directly into a BASIC program; instead, it should be entered as a command from the keyboard by the user.

INTERMEDIATE OUTPUT

In some instances, including intermediate PRINT statements as a part of the program may be preferable to using STOP statements and displaying the values of variables in Immediate mode.

Appropriate PRINT statements can be inserted after each statement or series of statements involving computations. This technique is called **source language debugging** or the **intermediate-output method**. Intermediate results are displayed until the specific portion of the program that is in error can be deduced.

If a program produces little output to begin with, the intermediate-output method should be used, since the outputs from the intermediate PRINT statements will be easy to distinguish from the regular output. If a program produces a great deal of output, then the technique involving the STOP, PRINT, and CONT statements should be used to minimize the amount of output to the display unit.

INDEX

MICROSOFT BASIC REFERENCE CARD

Legend: *Uppercase letters are required keywords. You must supply items within < > s. You must select one of the entries within { }'s. Items within [ ]'s are optional. Three ellipsis points (...) indicate that an item may be repeated as many times as you wish. The symbol ʙ represents a blank character.*

Summary of BASIC Statements

STATEMENT

BEEP
Causes the speaker on the computer to beep for one quarter of a second.

CHAIN <"filespec"> [,line number] [,ALL]
Instructs the computer to stop executing the current program, then load another program from auxiliary storage and start executing it.

CIRCLE <(x, y), radius> [,color [,start,end [,shape]]]
Causes the computer to draw an ellipse, circle, arc, or wedge with center at (x, y).

CLOSE [#] [filenumber] [,[#] [filenumber]]...
Closes specified files.

CLS
Erases the information on the first 24 lines of the screen and places the cursor in the upper left corner of the screen.

COLOR [background] [,palette]
In medium-resolution graphics mode, sets the color for the background and palette of colors.

COLOR [foreground] [,background] [,border]
In text mode, defines the color of the foreground characters, background, and border around the screen.

COM(n) {ON}{OFF}{STOP} Enables or disables trapping of communications activity on adaptor n.

COMMON <variable> [,variable]...
Passes specified variables to a chained program.

DATA <data item> [,data item]...
Provides for the creation of a sequence of data items for use by the READ statement.

DATE$ = mm {/}{-} dd {/}{-} yy[yy] Sets the system date, where mm = month, dd = day, yy = year, yyyy = 4-digit year.

DEF FN<name> [(variable [,variable]...)] = <expression>
Defines and names a function that can be referenced in a program as often as needed.

DIM <array name(size)> [,array name(size)]...
Reserves storage locations for arrays.

DRAW <string expression>
Causes the computer to draw the object that is defined by the value of the string expression.

STATEMENT

END
Terminates program execution and closes all opened files.

ERASE <array name> [,array name]...
Eliminates previously defined arrays.

FIELD <#filenumber, width AS string variable> [,width AS string variable]... Allocates space for variables in a random file buffer.

FOR numeric variable = initial TO limit [STEP increment]
Causes the statements between the FOR and NEXT statements to be executed repeatedly until the value of the numeric variable exceeds the value of the limit.

GET <(x$_1$, y$_1$) - (x$_2$, y$_2$), array name >
Reads the colors of the points in the specified area on the screen into an array.

GET [#][filenumber] [,record number]
Reads the specified record from a random file and transfers it to the buffer that is defined by the corresponding FIELD statement.

GOSUB <line number>
Causes control to transfer to the subroutine represented by the specified line number. Also retains the location of the next statement following the GOSUB statement.

GOTO <line number>
Causes an unconditional branch to the line number.

IF <condition> THEN [clause]
Causes execution of the THEN clause if the condition is true.

IF <condition> THEN [clause] ELSE [clause]
Causes execution of the THEN clause if the condition is true. Causes execution of the ELSE clause if the condition is false.

INPUT [;][;]"prompt message" {;}{,} <variable> [,variable]...
Provides for the assignment of values to variables from a source external to the program, like the keyboard.

INPUT <#filenumber, variable> [,variable]...
Provides for the assignment of values to variables from a sequential file in auxiliary storage.

KEY {ON}{OFF} Turns the display of the ten function keys on line 25 of the screen on or off.

KEY(n) {ON}{OFF}{STOP} Activates or deactivates trapping of the specified key n.

[LET] <variable> = <expression>
Causes the evaluation of the expression, followed by the assignment of the resulting value to the variable to the left of the equal sign.

LINE [(x$_1$, y$_1$)] -(x$_2$, y$_2$) [,color] [,B[F]] [,Style]
Draws a line or a box on the screen.

STATEMENT

**LINE INPUT [;][;]"prompt message"; <string variable> or
LINE INPUT <#filenumber,> <string variable>**
Provides for the assignment of a line up to 255 characters from a source external to the program, like the keyboard or a sequential file.

LOCATE [row] [,column] [,cursor] [,start] [,stop]
Positions the cursor on the screen. Can also be used to make the cursor visible or invisible and to control the size of the cursor.

LPRINT [item] [{;}{,} item]... Provides for the generation of output to the printer.

LPRINT USING <string expression;> <item> [{;}{,} item]...
Provides for the generation of formatted output to the printer.

LSET <string variable> = <string expression>
Moves string data left-justified into an area of a random file buffer that is defined by the string variable.

MID$ <(string var, start position [,number]> = <substring>
Replaces a substring within a string.

NEXT [numeric variable] [,numeric variable]...
Identifies the end of the For loop(s).

ON COM(n) GOSUB <line number>
Causes control to transfer to the line number when data is filling the communications buffer (n).

ON ERROR GOTO <line number>
Enables error trapping and specifies the first line to branch to in the event of an error. If the line number is zero, error trapping is disabled.

ON <numeric expression> GOSUB <line number> [,line number]... Causes control to transfer to the subroutine represented by the selected line number. Also retains the location of the next statement following the ON-GOSUB statement.

ON <numeric expression> GOTO <line number> [,line number]... Causes control to transfer to one of several line numbers according to the value of the numeric expression.

ON KEY(n) GOSUB <line number>
Causes control to transfer to the line number when the function key or cursor control key (n) is pressed.

ON PEN GOSUB <line number>
Causes control to transfer to the line number when the light pen is activated.

ON PLAY(n) GOSUB <line number>
Plays continuous background music. Transfers control to the line number when a note (n) is sensed.

(BASIC Statements *continued on page R.2 in left column*)

MICROSOFT BASIC REFERENCE CARD

Summary of BASIC Statements (continued)

STATEMENT

ON STRIG(n) GOSUB <line number>
Causes control to transfer to the line number when one of the joystick buttons (n) is pressed.

ON TIMER(n) GOSUB <line number>
Causes control to transfer to the line number when the specified period of time (n) in seconds has elapsed.

OPEN <filespec> FOR <mode> AS <[#]filenumber> [LEN = record length] or
OPEN <mode, [#]filenumber, filespec> [,record length]
Allows a program to read or write records to a file. If record length is specified, then the file is opened as a random file. If the record length is not specified, then the file is opened as a sequential file.

OPTION BASE $\begin{Bmatrix} 0 \\ 1 \end{Bmatrix}$ Assigns a lower bound of 0 to 1 to all arrays.

PAINT <(x, y)> [[,paint] [,boundary]]
Paints an area on the screen with the selected color.

PEN $\begin{Bmatrix} \text{ON} \\ \text{OFF} \\ \text{STOP} \end{Bmatrix}$ Enables or disables the PEN read function used to analyze light pen activity.

PLAY <string expression >
Causes the computer to play music according to the value of the string expression.

PRESET <(x, y)> [,color]
Draws a point in the color specified at (x, y). If no color is specified, it erases the point.

$\begin{Bmatrix} \text{PRINT} \\ ? \end{Bmatrix}$ [item] $\left[\begin{Bmatrix} , \\ ; \end{Bmatrix} \text{[item]} \right]$... Provides for the generation of output to the screen.

$\begin{Bmatrix} \text{PRINT} \\ ? \end{Bmatrix}$ <#filenumber,> [item] $\left[\begin{Bmatrix} , \\ ; \end{Bmatrix} \text{[item]} \right]$...
Provides for the generation of output to a sequential file.

PRINT USING <string expression:> <item>[$\begin{Bmatrix} , \\ ; \end{Bmatrix}$ [item]...
Provides for the generation of formatted output to the screen.

PRINT <#filenumber,> USING <string expression:>
<item>[$\begin{Bmatrix} , \\ ; \end{Bmatrix}$ [item]... Provides for the generation of formatted output to a sequential file

PSET <(x, y)> [,color]
Draws a point in the color specified at (x, y).

PUT <(x₁, y₁), array name> [,action]
Writes the colors of the points in the array onto an area of the screen.

STATEMENT

PUT <[#]filenumber> [,record number]
Writes a record to a random file from a buffer defined by the corresponding FIELD statement.

RANDOMIZE [numeric expression]
Reseeds the random number generator.

READ <variable> [,variable]...
Provides for the assignment of values to variables from a sequence of data items created from DATA statements.

$\begin{Bmatrix} \text{REM} \\ ' \end{Bmatrix}$ [comment] Provides for the insertion of comments in a program.

RESTORE [line number]
Allows the data items in DATA statements to be reread.

RESUME $\begin{Bmatrix} \text{line number} \\ \text{NEXT} \\ 0 \\ b \end{Bmatrix}$ Continues program execution at the line number, or the line following that which caused the error, after an error-recovery procedure.

RETURN [line number]
Causes control to transfer from a subroutine back to the statement that follows the corresponding GOSUB or ON-GOSUB statement.

RSET <string variable > = <string expression >
Moves string data right-justified into an area of a random file buffer that is defined by string variable.

SCREEN [mode] [,color switch] [,active page] [,visual page]
Sets the screen attributes for text mode, medium-resolution graphics, or high-resolution graphics.

SOUND <frequency, duration >
Causes the generation of sound through the computer speaker.

STOP
Stops execution of a program. Unlike the END statement, files are left open.

STRIG(n) $\begin{Bmatrix} \text{ON} \\ \text{OFF} \\ \text{STOP} \end{Bmatrix}$ Enables or disables trapping of the joystick buttons.

SWAP <variable, variable,>
Exchanges the values of two variables or two elements of an array.

TIME$ = hh[:mm[:ss]]
Sets the system time where hh = hours, mm = minutes, and ss = seconds.

TIMER $\begin{Bmatrix} \text{ON} \\ \text{OFF} \\ \text{STOP} \end{Bmatrix}$ Enables or disables trapping of timed events.

VIEW [[SCREEN] <(x₁, y₁) – (x₂, y₂)>] [,color] [,boundary]
Defines a viewport.

STATEMENT

WEND
Identifies the end of a While loop.

WHILE <condition >
Identifies the beginning of a While loop. Causes the statements between WHILE and WEND to be executed repeatedly while the condition is true.

WIDTH $\begin{Bmatrix} 40 \\ 80 \end{Bmatrix}$ Erases the information on the first 24 lines of the screen, sets the width of the line on the screen to 40 or 80 characters, and places the cursor in the upper left corner of the screen.

WINDOW <[SCREEN] (x₁, y₁) – (x₂, y₂) >
Redefines the coordinates of the viewport. Allows you to draw objects in space and not be bounded by the limits of the screen.

WRITE [expression list]
Writes data to the screen. Identical to the PRINT statement except that it causes commas to be inserted between items displayed; causes strings to be delimited with quotation marks; and positive numbers are not preceded by blanks.

WRITE <#filenumber,> [item] $\left[\begin{Bmatrix} , \\ ; \end{Bmatrix} \text{[item]} \right]$...
Writes data to a sequential file. Causes the computer to insert commas between the items written to the sequential file.

Summary of BASIC Commands

COMMAND

AUTO [line number] [,increment]
Automatically starts a BASIC line with a line number. Each new line is assigned a systematically incremented line number.

CLEAR
Assigns all numeric variables the value zero and all string variables the null value.

CONT
Resumes a system activity, like the execution of a program, following interruption due to pressing the Control and Break keys simultaneously or execution of the STOP or END statement.

DELETE [lineno₁] [-lineno₂]
Deletes line numbers lineno₁ through lineno₂ in the current program.

EDIT <line number>
Displays a line for editing purposes.

FILES ["device name:]
Lists the names of all programs and data files in auxiliary storage as specified by the device name.

(BASIC Commands *continued on page R 3 in left column*)

MICROSOFT BASIC REFERENCE CARD

Summary of BASIC Commands (continued)

COMMAND

KILL <"filespec">
Deletes a previously stored program or data file from auxiliary storage.

LIST [line number,] [−line number,] [,"filespec]
Causes all or part of the BASIC program currently in main memory to be displayed on the screen. The LIST command can also be used to copy lines to a file in auxiliary storage.

LLIST [line number,] [−line number,]
Causes all or part of the BASIC program currently in main memory to be displayed on the printer.

LOAD <"filespec>
Loads a previously stored program from auxiliary storage into main memory.

MERGE <"filespec>
Merges the lines from a program in auxiliary storage with the program in main memory. The program in main memory or storage must have been saved using the A (ASCII) parameter.

NAME <"old filespec"> AS <"new filespec">
Changes the name of a program or data file in auxiliary storage to a new name.

NEW
Causes the BASIC program currently in main memory to be erased and indicates the beginning of a new program to be created in main memory.

RENUM [new line number] [,[old line number] [,increment]]
Renumbers the program uniformly with a new line number and increment.

RUN { line number / "filespec" [",R] }
Causes the BASIC program currently in main memory to be executed. This command can also be used to begin execution at a specified line number of the program in main memory or to load and execute a program from auxiliary storage.

SAVE <"filespec> [,A]
Saves the current program into auxiliary storage for later use. The parameter A instructs the computer to save the file in character format (ASCII) rather than binary format.

SHELL
Places the current BASICA session in a temporary wait state and returns control to the operating system MS DOS. When the operating system prompt appears, you can enter MS DOS commands. To return to the BASICA session, type EXIT.

SYSTEM
Causes the computer to permanently exit BASICA and return control to the operating system MS DOS.

TROFF
Turns off the program trace feature.

COMMAND

TRON
Turns on the program trace feature.

Summary of BASIC Functions

FUNCTION

ABS(N)
Returns the absolute value of the argument N.

ASC(X$)
Returns a two-digit numeric value that is equivalent in ASCII code to the first character of the string argument X$.

ATN(N)
Returns the angle in radians whose tangent is the value of the argument N.

CHR$(N)
Returns a single string character that is equivalent in ASCII code to the numeric argument N.

COS(N)
Returns the cosine of the argument N where N is in radians.

CVI(X$), CVS(X$), CVD(X$)
Returns the integer, single-precision, or double-precision numeric value equivalent to the string X$. Used with random files.

EOF(filenumber)
Returns −1 (true) if the end of file has been sensed on the sequential file associated with filenumber. Returns 0 (false) if the end of file has not been sensed.

EXP(N)
Returns e(2.718281...) raised to the argument N.

FIX(N)
Returns the value of N truncated to an integer.

FRE(N)
Returns the number of unused bytes within BASIC's data space. N is a dummy argument.

INPUT$(N)
Suspends execution of the program until a string of N characters is received from the keyboard.

INSTR([P,] X$, S$)
Returns the beginning position of the substring S$ in string X$. P indicates the position at which the search begins in the string X$.

INT(N)
Returns the largest integer that is less than or equal to the argument N.

LEFT$(X$, N)
Returns the leftmost N characters of the string argument X$.

FUNCTION

LEN(X$)
Returns the length of the string argument X$.

LOC(#filenumber)
With a random file, it returns the number of the last record read or written. With a sequential file, it returns the number of records read from or written to the file.

LOF(#filenumber)
Returns the number of bytes allocated to a file.

LOG(N)
Returns the natural log of the argument N where N is greater than 0.

MID$(X$, P, N)
Returns N characters of the string argument X$ beginning at position P.

MKI$(N), MKS$(N), MKD$(N)
Returns the string equivalent of an integer, single-precision or double-precision value. Used with random files.

PEN(n)
Reads the light pen.

PLAY(n)
Returns the number of notes currently in the music background buffer.

PMAP (c, n)
Returns the world coordinate of the physical coordinate c or vice versa. The parameter n varies between 0 and 3 and determines whether c is an x or y coordinate and whether the coordinate is to be mapped from the physical to the world coordinate or vice versa.

POINT { (x, y) / (n) }
With the argument (x, y), the computer returns the foreground color attribute of the point (x, y). With the argument n, the computer returns the physical or world x or y coordinate of the last point referenced. The parameter n varies in the range 0 to 3.

POS(N)
Returns the current position of the cursor on the screen. N is a dummy argument.

RIGHT$(X$, N)
Returns the rightmost N characters of the string argument X$.

RND(N)
Returns a random number between 0 (inclusive) and 1 (exclusive). If N is positive or not included, the next random number is returned. If N is 0 (zero), the previous random number is returned. If N is negative, the random number generator is reseeded before a random number is returned.

SCREEN(row., column)
Returns the ASCII code for the character at the specified row (line) and column on the screen.

(BASIC Functions continued on page R 4 in left column)

MICROSOFT BASIC REFERENCE CARD

Summary of BASIC Functions (continued)

FUNCTION

SGN(N)
Returns the sign of the argument N: −1 if the argument N is less than 0, 0 if the argument N is equal to 0, or +1 if the argument N is greater than 0.

SIN(N)
Returns the sine of the argument N where N is in radians.

SPACE$(N)
Returns a string of N spaces.

SPC(N)
Displays N spaces. Can be used only in an output statement, like PRINT or LPRINT.

SQR(N)
Returns the square root of the positive argument N.

STR$(N)
Returns the string equivalent of the numeric argument N.

STRIG(n)
Returns the status of the joystick buttons.

STRING$(N, X$)
Returns N times the first character of X$.

TAB(N)
Causes the computer to tab over to position N on the output device. Can be used only in an output statement, like PRINT or LPRINT.

TAN(N)
Returns the tangent of the argument N where N is in radians.

TIMER
Returns a value that is equal to the number of seconds elapsed since midnight.

VAL(X$)
Returns the numeric equivalent of the string argument X$.

Summary of Special Variables

VARIABLE

CSRLIN
Equal to the vertical (row) coordinate of the cursor.

DATE$
Equal to the current date (mm-dd-yyyy).

ERL
Equal to the line number of the last error. Used for error trapping.

ERR
Equal to the error code of the last error. Used for error trapping.

VARIABLE

INKEY$
Equal to the last character entered from the keyboard

TIME$
Equal to the current time (hh:mm:ss).

Summary of All Operators

ORDER OF PRECEDENCE	*OPERATOR*	*SYMBOL*
Highest	**Arithmetic**	^
		− (Unary minus sign)
		* or /
		MOD
		+ or −
	Concatenation	+
	Relational	=, >, > =, <, < =, or <>
	Logical	NOT
		AND
		OR or XOR
		EQV
Lowest		IMP

Microsoft BASIC Reserved Words

ABS	DEF	GOSUB	LPOS	POS	STICK
AND	DEFDBL	GOTO	LPRINT	PRESET	STOP
ASC	DEFINT	HEX$	LSET	PRINT	STR$
ATN	DEFSNG	IF	MERGE	PRINT#	STRIG
AUTO	DEFSTR	IMP	MID$	PSET	STRING$
BEEP	DELETE	INKEY$	MKDIR	PUT	SWAP
BLOAD	DIM	INP	MKD$	RANDOMIZE	SYSTEM
BSAVE	DRAW	INPUT	MKI$	READ	TAB(
CALL	EDIT	INPUT#	MKS$	REM	TAN
CDBL	ELSE	INPUT$	MOD	RENUM	THEN
CHAIN	END	INSTR	MOTOR	RESET	TIMER
CHDIR	ENVIRON	INT	NAME	RESTORE	TIMES
CHR$	ENVIRON$	INTER$	NEW	RESUME	TO
CINT	EOF	IOCTL	NEXT	RETURN	TROFF
CIRCLE	EQV	IOCTL$	NOT	RIGHT$	TRON
CLEAR	ERASE	KEY	OCT$	RMDIR	USING
CLOSE	ERDEV	KEYS	OFF	RND	USR
CLS	ERDEV$	KILL	ON	RSET	VAL
COLOR	ERL	LEFT$	OPEN	RUN	VARPTR
COM	ERR	LEN	OPTION	SAVE	VARPTR$
COMMON	ERROR	LET	OR	SCREEN	VIEW
CONT	EXP	LINE	OUT	SGN	WAIT
COS	FIELD	LIST	PAINT	SHELL	WEND
CSRLIN	FILES	LLIST	PEEK	SIN	WHILE
CVD	FIX	LOAD	PEN	SOUND	WIDTH
CVI	FNcccccccc	LOC	PLAY	SPACE$	WINDOW
CVS	FOR	LOCATE	PMAP	SPC(	WRITE
DATA	FRE	LOF	POINT	SQR	WRITE#
DATE$	GET	LOG	POKE	STEP	XOR

Summary of Special Keys

KEYS	*FUNCTION*
Caps Lock	Acts as a toggle switch for changing the keyboard to uppercase or lowercase mode. Nonletter keys are not affected.
Ctrl + Alt + Delete	Resets the computer. Used to *warm start* (i.e. reboot) the computer.
Ctrl + Break	Terminates a computer activity, like the execution of a program, automatic line numbering, or the listing of a program.
Ctrl + End	Erases from the cursor position to the end of the current line.
Ctrl + Enter	Inserts blanks through the end of the current line.
Ctrl + Home	Clears the screen and places the cursor in the upper left corner of the screen.
Ctrl + Num Lock	Stops the computer. Press any key (except Shift, Break, or Insert) to resume.
Ctrl + Print Screen	Acts as a toggle on/off switch. Directs output to the printer as well as the screen.
Delete	Deletes the character at the cursor position on the screen.
End	Moves the cursor to the end of the line.
Esc	Cancels any changes to the current line.
Home	Moves the cursor to the upper left corner of the screen.
Insert	Enters or exits Insert mode.
Num Lock	Acts as a toggle switch to turn the numeric keypad on or off.
Shift + Print Screen	Prints the contents of the screen onto a printer.
Spacebar	Transmits a blank character and advances the cursor one position to the right.
Shift	Causes characters pressed while this key is held down to be displayed in uppercase form (lowercase if the keyboard is in uppercase mode).
Backspace	Backspaces the cursor one position and erases the character to the left of the cursor.
Enter	Enters a line and places the cursor in position 1 of the next line.
→ ← ↑ ↓	The four arrow keys move the cursor in the indicated directions.
Tab	Moves the cursor to the next tab position. Inserts eight blanks in Insert mode.